Construction Materials For Interior Design

Construction Materials For Interior Design

Principles of Structure and Properties of Materials

William Rupp with Arnold Friedmann
Drawings by Philip Farrell

WHITNEY LIBRARY OF DESIGN
an imprint of Watson-Guptill Publications/New York

First published in New York by Whitney Library of Design
an imprint of Watson-Guptill Publications
a division of Billboard Publications, Inc.
1515 Broadway, New York, NY 10036

Library of Congress Cataloging-in-Publication Data

Rupp, William E.
   Construction materials for interior design.

   Includes index.
   1. Building materials.   2. Interior architecture.
I. Friedmann, Arnold.   II. Title.
TA403.6.R76   1989   747'.028   88-33768
ISBN 0-8230-0929-7
ISBN 0-8230-0930-0 (pbk.)

Manufactured in U.S.A.

First printing, 1989

1 2 3 4 5 6 7 8 9 / 94 93 92 91 90 89

Contents

Foreword

Interior design has reached professional maturity, but this has not ended the debate about what it precisely constitutes. This question most likely will never be resolved to the satisfaction of everyone, and perhaps that is a good thing. If we can agree that all design fields are creative professions, it would also appear desirable to agree to the fact that overly specialized divisions of the larger field dealing with the environment are not really desirable. Interior design merges with architecture, and much of what interior designers do is interior architecture. Where interior design begins and where architecture ends is an unresolved question. I believe that the best projects are those where one cannot tell the difference, and where the interiors have been designed in total sympathy with the architecture, whether by the architect or by an interior designer.

Clearly, interior designers need to understand the structures in which they work. They need not know all of the engineering aspects; they do not require the technical expertise expected of architects, but certainly they must be familiar with the basic approach to structure; and they must understand the properties of the materials that have been used to construct a building.

Since there is universal agreement about this need to understand, most schools and universities offering programs in interior design include some instruction in building construction. While interior design education differs from architectural education in a number of respects, these differences are largely a matter of scope and scale. Interior designers need to concentrate on the near environment; color, texture, finish materials, lighting, and furnishings. These aspects of the interior must be dealt with more than structure and building technology. Nevertheless, the qualifying examination given in interior design by NCIDQ (National Council for Interior Design Qualification) expects an understanding of materials and principles of construction.

I was fortunate to be associated with one of the first programs that had a strong orientation toward interior architecture during the sixties, as Associate Chair of the Department of Interior Design at Pratt Institute. Interior materials and construction were very much part of that curriculum, although we experienced some difficulties in finding the right people to teach the subject. We found it even more difficult to select the appropriate texts. It seemed obvious that architects were the logical choice to fill these teaching positions. Many architects, however, find it difficult to relate to the somewhat different requirements and expectations of interior design students. A highly technical approach presupposes a background in mathematics and physics, which most interior design students do not have. Sometimes there is the temptation to talk down to students lacking an architecture background, resulting in negative attitudes on the part of students. The texts used in such courses are written for architectural or engineering students and are therefore too technical and, often, boring to students who are more interested in design and aesthetics.

This problem of finding staff and appropriate course materials was true also at the University of Massachusetts, where I have been on the faculty since 1972. We considered ourselves very fortunate when William Rupp joined our faculty in 1976 as a part-time instructor. In the ensuing years he became a full-time faculty member and has developed several construction courses for our interior design program. Bill Rupp brought many years of high-level professional experience to his teaching, with a knowledge of construction and materials that is encyclopedic. Above all, he comprehends, better than anyone else I have worked with, the approach that makes the understanding of materials of construction an interesting subject for interior design students. Most of these students have gone on to become very successful designers. The fact that our students are very much in demand is to a large extent due to the fact that they have an excellent background in architectural construction in addition to their design education.

For a number of years, Bill Rupp searched for the right text for his courses, accumulating more textbooks on construction and materials than anyone I know. Since I have been involved with the NCIDQ for many years and am aware of the national need for a concise text on materials of construction for interior design, I urged Bill Rupp to write such a book and agreed to help. I was also able to enlist the aid of Philip Farrell, a leading delineator and illustrator. Phil Farrell is an excellent and experienced interior designer and has taught at Pratt Institute for the past fourteen years.

We did not set out to write the definitive text on materials of construction for interior design. But by putting our joint experience together, we decided that we could write a text that would give students the basic understanding of materials of construction that an interior designer must have. This book is written to be easily read and understood. It is illustrated with many details that will be helpful to interior designers. We expect this book to be of use as a major study resource for those preparing for the NCIDQ examination. Finally, we hope that the book will be a welcome and ongoing reference for practicing interior designers at any stage in their professional careers.

Arnold Friedmann

Preface

When a book such as this is conceived, one finds that there is a nearly limitless resource of information available. The overwhelming problem lies in deciding what should be included and what may be omitted. Available texts too often dwell on the technology of manufacture and too little on the appearance and use of materials. My favorite example is the full-page illustration of a pug mill, which could as well be a picture of a diesel locomotive. I have chosen to elaborate on manufacture only when the process affects the finished appearance of the material, or as an explanation for a peculiar name.

There is included, however, a certain amount of historical background for those materials that have been around long enough to have a history. This area is of more than casual interest, for it may aid the sense of appropriate use. One of the keys to good design resides in the appropriate use of materials. Anything that can bring a designer into a closer understanding of the nature of materials must be helpful.

The responsibility for most of the technical information is mine, based principally upon a lifetime as an architect and hands-on builder, and upon years of trying to teach building technology to interior design students. This material is presented as objectively as is possible for me. The subsections entitled "[Material] in Interiors" were written by my colleague, Dr. Arnold Friedmann, with no pretension whatever of objectivity. He brings a lifetime as an interior designer to bear, as well as half a lifetime as an educator; objectivity is not his intention for these sections.

It was decided in the beginning that photographs were often unclear and that good, crisp drawings were much better illustrations for a work of this nature. It was without hesitation that we turned to the talented Philip Farrell for such drawings. Mr. Farrell had demonstrated his capabilities in an earlier book of Dr. Friedmann's and brings to his work long experience as a practicing interior designer.

No material can ever be completely objective or wholly accurate; if any of our prejudices, errors, or omissions seem too gross to be overlooked, we welcome a word from our readers.

William Rupp

1 A Structural Primer

In the broadest and simplest of terms, structure may be defined as the elements of a building forming a building's resistance to forces that are in opposition to its stability, such as gravity, wind, and seismic movements.

Structure through the Ages

Stones piled up for shelter from the wind by a people about 300,000 years ago on the French Riviera are taken to be the earliest known deliberate structures created by humans. While stone may not be the oldest structural material used, it is the most durable and has left us a record of the progression of structural concepts from the earliest times.

The oldest extant space-spanning structures are the stone lintels of ancient Egyptian temples. Unable to calculate the stresses involved, and given the unreliable nature of stone, the Egyptians used spans that were very short, seldom exceeding the diameter of the columns themselves. A great hall, therefore, was nearly filled with columns. This structural system has been labeled post-and-lintel construction. The name has adhered although modern terminology would prefer column and beam.

When they reached for grandeur, the early Mesopotamian civilizations, with no stone available, could only reach for the clay at their feet. With clay in the form of brick, they learned to make small elements span great distances. At first the bricks were made to overhang each course below until they met at the top, forming a corbeled arch. The true arch was born when it was learned to make the bricks wedge shaped and arrange them around the axis of a semicircular formwork. Such an assemblage cannot fail unless one of the wedges is dislodged. When the arch is extended along its axis, a vault is created. Rotate the arch about its center and a dome is formed. Despite much sophistication in many respects, the builders of the great pre-Columbian Central American cities never discovered the true arch, nor did they develop the wheel, the concepts for both of which are similar. They had to settle for corbeled vaults to create the narrow open spaces within their great monuments.

POST AND LINTEL

CORBELED ARCH, TRUE ARCH, VAULT, DOME

CORBELED ARCH

DOME

TRUE ARCH

VAULT

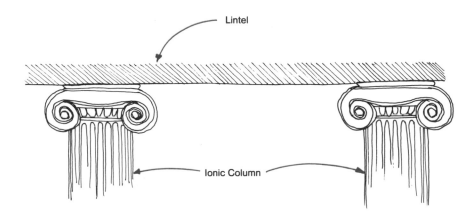

The Greeks improved upon the Egyptian structure only slightly. With fine quality marble and greater daring they increased the span of their lintels to one and a half and even two times the diameter of the column. Ornamental as classical column capitals became, their prime function was still to reduce the span of the lintel.

The ancient Romans inherited the art of the arch from the cities of Asia and spanned great spaces with arches, vaults, and domes. To let in more light, cross vaulting was developed, in which two or more vaults rested on great masonry piers. This art was brought to the highest expression with the vast lofty cathedrals of the Middle Ages.

Despite the unquestionable grandeur of these buildings, structural engineering, a mathematical discipline, had not yet been born. Mathematics had been raised to a great science, but stood aloof from practical application. The first architects relied upon the trial-and-error experience of centuries (the title "architect" is derived from the Greek "architekton," for master builder).

Modern structural design emerged in the nineteenth century, not originally from mathematics, but from the pragmatic testing of structural materials. Thus the beginning course in structural design is "Strength of Materials." When this information, derived from tests, had been sufficiently compiled, mathematical formulas could be devised, creating the discipline now called "statics." This is the study of forces in balance, and, therefore, motionless. In structural design this is a condition much to be desired, as movement is often the first, if not always the last, sign of structural failure. This discipline developed in response to the emergence of new structural materials in the Industrial Revolution. Iron and steel had been available for millennia, but their high cost and scarcity limited their use to tools and weapons. With the advent of the

Industrial Revolution these materials were produced in such quantities that it became possible to use them for building structure. At about the same time, portland cement was invented, enabling masons to create concrete, a material known to the Romans but forgotten during the Dark Ages. The combination of steel and concrete produced the ultimate twentieth-century structural material: reinforced concrete.

The first structural use of iron was for columns in mill buildings, which eliminated space-consuming interior masonry piers and load-bearing walls. A standard type of mill construction developed with brick exterior walls, cast iron columns, heavy timber beams, and plank flooring. Soon the casting of modular iron panels for the exterior faces of buildings became possible. The relative light weight of the panels reduced the dead load of masonry structure, while the thinness of the material saved additional space. But the great interest in cast iron building fronts, in an age of classical revival, was generated by the ability they offered to repeatedly cast the fine classical details very much in demand at the time. By 1851 it was possible for Thomas Paxton to build his Crystal Palace in London entirely of iron framework. By the time the Brooklyn Bridge was started in 1867, steel, with its great tensile strength, had established itself as the master structural material.

STRUCTURAL STEEL FRAME

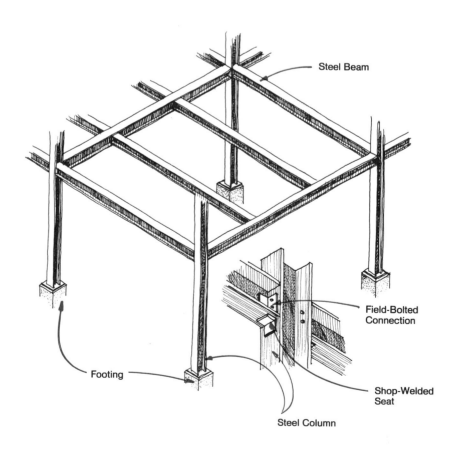

Steel Beam

Field-Bolted Connection

Shop-Welded Seat

Footing

Steel Column

The combination of steel and concrete as a unified structure followed the use of concrete as fire protection for steel. Reinforced concrete as a structural material with inherent aesthetic potential was first explored by Auguste Perret shortly after the turn of the century. Further pragmatic testing of reinforced concrete elements permitted more precise formulas to be devised, and raised its manufacture to a reliable science. Such masters as Pier Luigi Nervi have demonstrated the outer limits of the minimum material required to span a distance and the beauty achievable through structural analysis.

Steel has been by no means neglected during this development; indeed, the majority of high-rise structures are still steel frame. In contemporary structures the tensile values of this metal are put into full play by modern cable suspension roofs and the anchoring of air-support structures. These follow the beautiful catenary curve, the natural curve followed by a flexible cord hanging from two fixed points.

Strength and Stress

Tensile strength is only one of the qualities of a structural material required to resist the forces that act upon it. Stress is the internal reaction of a structural member to an external force. Structural design begins with the determination of these stresses and the selection of members capable of enduring them.

Since stresses are the result of the loads imposed upon a structure, the loads that are to be expected must be given some consideration. They are defined as a combination of dead and live loads.

Dead loads are composed of the very stuff of the building: the weight of all the materials of the structure, infilling, and finish materials, expressed in pounds per square foot (or kilograms per square meter). All materials must be identified and their weights obtained from tables or by calculation and added together.

Live loads begin with the loads on the roof, according to climate (snow and/or wind), and floors, according to the occupancy or use. The designer must determine the occupancy of each floor of the building, then consult the appropriate building code section for the required live loads. Since this information is determined only by code, the designer must determine, from the outset of a project, the agency with jurisdiction over the work and the particular building code that is the authority. There are many building codes, and only recently have they been tending toward uniformity. Given regional variations in climate, frequency and severity of storms, and history of earthquakes, regional codes may always be with us.

Load factors due to wind or earthquake must also be obtained from the pertinent codes. These loads become more important in higher buildings. In skyscrapers these loads dominate those of the occupancy.

OCCUPANCY OR USE	LIVE LOAD (PSF)
Assembly halls and other places of assembly:	
Fixed seats	60
Movable seats	100
Balcony (exterior):	
One- and two-family dwellings only	60
Court rooms	100
Corridors:	
First floor	100
Other floors, same as occupancy served	
Dance halls and ballrooms	100
Dining rooms and restaurants	100
Garages (passenger cars only)	50
Gymnasiums, main floors and balconies	100
Hospitals:	
Operating rooms, laboratories	60
Private rooms	40
Wards	40
Corridors, above first floor	80
Manufacturing:	
Light	125
Heavy	250
Office buildings:	
Offices	50
Lobbies	100
Corridors, above first floor	80

OCCUPANCY OR USE	LIVE LOAD (PSF)
Open parking structures (passenger cars only)	50
Residential:	
Multifamily houses	
Private apartments	40
Public rooms	100
Corridors	80
Dwellings	
First floor	40
Second floor and habitable attics	30
Hotels	
Guest rooms	40
Public rooms	100
Corridors	80
Schools:	
Classrooms	50
Corridors	100
Stairs and exitways	100
Storage warehouse:	
Light	125
Heavy	250
Stores:	
Retail	
First floor, rooms	100
Upper floors	75
Wholesale	125
Theaters:	
Aisles, corridors, and lobbies	100
Orchestra floors	60
Balconies	60
Stage floors	150

Dead loads are always cumulative, starting with the roof and going down: the wall below the roof, the top floor, the next wall, the next floor, and so forth until the foundation load has been determined. On high-rise buildings the live load may be reduced by given factors, on the assumption that not all floors will be loaded to the maximum at all times.

Sometimes the combination of loads acting in a vertical direction (gravity) and those acting in a horizontal direction (wind and earth-quake) combine to form a force acting at an angle between. This is called the vector of the forces. The vector can be determined by a simple graphic process.

VECTOR OF FORCES

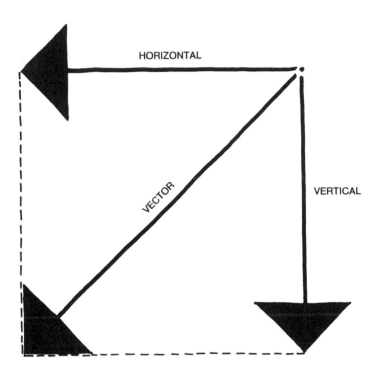

It is in the nature of materials to suffer change of shape under the impact of external forces. This change of shape is called deformation. It is this deformation that creates the internal stresses that must be resisted by the material to maintain a stable structure. These deformations may not be visible to the eye; on the other hand, a noticeably sagging beam may not represent structural failure, if it is within allowable limits.

There may be a number of forces at work in concert upon a structural material, resulting in various stresses. Compressive stress is the result of a load bearing directly upon a material, tending to crush it.

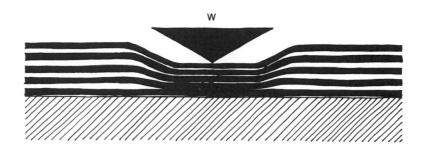

It must be imagined that the material resists this force by its inherent stability, otherwise the object under compression would move and there would be no static condition.

Different materials have varied ability to resist compressive stress: Stone and concrete are relatively high; wood is less so but higher against the end grain than across the grain. Steel is highest of all. Compressive stress may be the result of simple load bearing, such as a column or wall; it is also a factor in bending stress, which is described on page 20.

When forces attempt to pull a material apart it is subject to tensile stress. In this respect many materials strong in compression, such as stone and concrete, are not strong in tension. Wood is relatively strong in tension and, again, steel is the strongest of all.

Tensile stress may exist in an uncomplicated way, as in suspension structures or in the ties of trusses. It is, like compression, also a factor in bending stress.

TENSILE STRENGTH

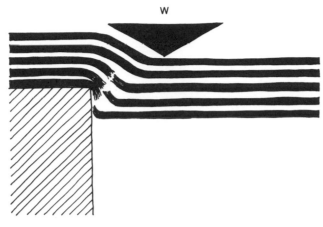

VERTICAL SHEAR

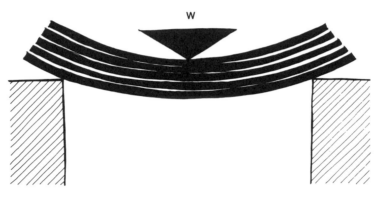

HORIZONTAL SHEAR

Shear stress may be another structural concern. Perhaps the correct word is stresses because there are two forms: horizontal and vertical shear. Vertical shear occurs in its simplest form when one end of a loaded beam is bearing on a column. It is easy to imagine the forces trying to cut vertically through the beam at this point. Horizontal shear is the stress tending to split a material lengthwise under the deformation of bending.

The bending deformation in a simple beam (one supported at the ends) generates a more complex stress pattern, known as bending stress. The bottom of the beam must stretch, causing tensile stress. The top of the beam attempts to become shorter, creating compressive stress. If the bottom is in tension and the top is in compression, it follows that somewhere in the middle the stresses must change and pass through zero stress. Indeed, this is what happens and that center plane is called the neutral axis. The stresses are greatest at the top and bottom, which are referred to as the extreme fibers, and diminish steadily toward the center.

It should be evident that economy suggests that the material for the beam should be concentrated at the top and bottom, the points of greatest stress. So it clearly is in the case of a typical steel beam and in the wood fabrication called a box beam.

SIMPLE BEAM AND BEAM STRESS DIAGRAM

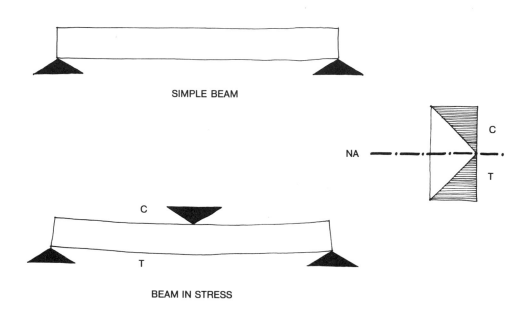

SIMPLE BEAM

BEAM IN STRESS

BOX BEAM AND I BEAM

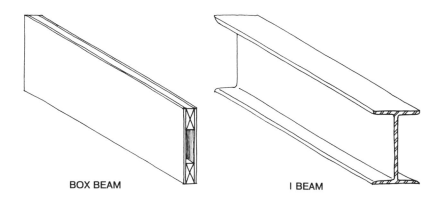

BOX BEAM

I BEAM

Here we can see that these beams have minimized the material between the areas of greatest stress. The material in the middle cannot be eliminated entirely, however. In the first place, the two stressed surfaces, called the flanges, must be held in correct relationship to each other. In the second place, the middle, called the web, must resist the stress of horizontal shear. This latter stress is seldom very critical except in the case of a short span that is heavily loaded. Resistance to bending is usually the major consideration in beam design. Different materials have inherently different degrees of stiffness, which can be indexed and then called the modulus of elasticity. To be structurally useful, this stiffness must be combined with elasticity. Plain concrete is very stiff but weak in tension; it fractures rather than bends. As a result, wood is much better and steel is far better yet as a beam material.

Besides the inherent qualities of the material, a major factor in stiffness resides in the shape of the structural member. This is referred to as the moment of inertia. In general, the deeper beam of the same mass is stiffer than the shallower beam because the distance between the neutral axis and the extreme fiber acts as a lever arm. A beam that is made too tall and thin, in order to improve the shape factor, cannot be made to take extreme advantage of this shape factor, like a ribbon on edge, because of the tendency of the top to flop over in the middle, which is called horizontal deflection. Most beams wind up being about twice as deep as they are wide, unless they are specially supported in the center.

The compressive forces bearing on a column tend to bend it in the direction of its weakest axis. Therefore, the ideal column shape is the cylinder, which has the same shape in all directions. Cylinders are not always the most convenient shape, however, so a square tube is often substituted, or the very wide flanged H beam.

Wood and steel, because they are about the same strength in tension and compression, are referred to as homogeneous structural materials. The same amount of material is required at the top and bottom of the beam. From another point of view, such a beam will work just as well upside down, and a normal structural member will be symmetrical about the vertical and horizontal axes. The neutral axis will be in the center, which is the right place to bore holes, if needed. There are also nonhomogeneous structural materials (no one seems to have decided to call them heterogeneous structures). These are composite structural systems made of materials with different characteristics, with the aim being to utilize the best characteristics of each.

Examples of such hybrid structures date from centuries back, when iron or steel rods were used to tie the haunches of masonry arches to absorb their thrust. Steel rods have long been in use as ties in wooden trusses, and are still so used today. Steel plates may be bolted between wooden members to build "flitched" beams. The ultimate non-homogeneous structural system is reinforced concrete, which combines

RELATIVE STIFFNESS OF SHAPES

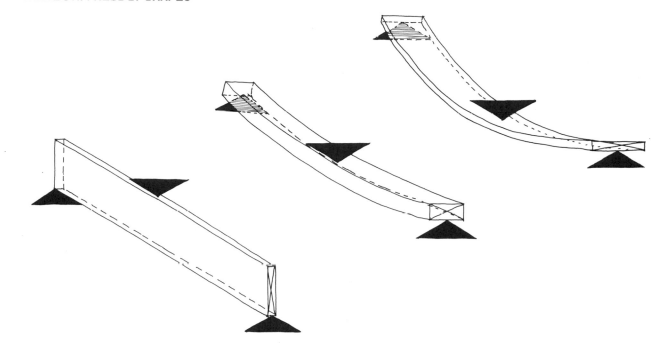

CYLINDER, SQUARE, AND H COLUMNS

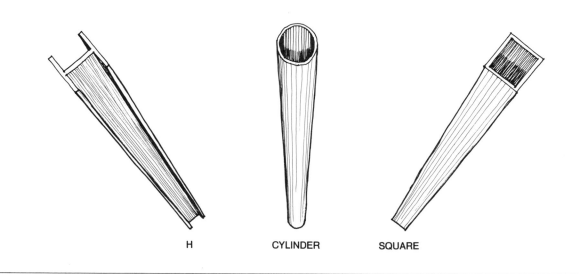

H   CYLINDER   SQUARE

the good compressive stress resistance of concrete with the high tensile strength of steel. In the case of a simple reinforced concrete beam, steel rods are placed near the bottom of the beam to resist the bulk of the tensile stresses. The concrete top surface endures all of the compressive stresses. The neutral axis finds its place at the point of balance between the center of the steel and the top of the concrete. Seldom is reinforced concrete used in so simple a manner, however. The fact that concrete can be poured to form many columns and beams simultaneously, with interlocking steel reinforcement, can create a continuous frame structure—a unified structural entity.

CONCRETE BEAM WITH REBAR

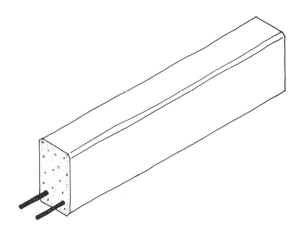

CONTINUOUS FRAME STRUCTURE

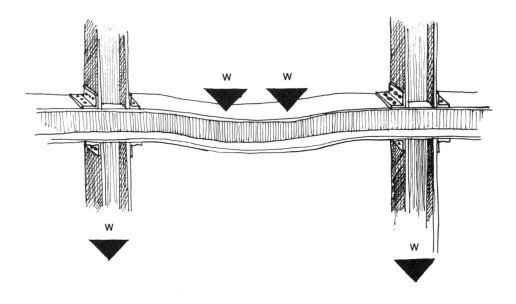

Continuous frame structures unify all of the members of a structural frame. Stress analysis for these structures is quite complex. A beam passing over a column will transfer its compressive stress and some of its bending stress from the top to the bottom of the column at that point. In fact, loading one member of a structural frame will transfer some of its stress to all the rest of the frame. However, this difficult design is worth the trouble because the structure will require less material than simple, or separate, beams and columns.

It is easy to see that in the construction of continuous frames the joints between members become critical. In steel structures the unification of the frame members is normally accomplished by welding all the joints. In concrete structures this task is rather more easily accomplished. The steel reinforcing bars can be run continuously between all of the members, effectively making the concrete one piece throughout.

The principle of using the least material for the greatest structural capability first reached a peak with the development of the truss. Basically, a truss is composed of an upper member, the top chord, in compression and a lower member, the bottom chord, in tension. They are connected by diagonals alternately in tension, called ties, and in compression, called struts. The struts and ties compose the web, which is always divided into triangles. Triangles assure rigidity because no angle can be changed in a triangle without changing the length of at least one of its sides.

The simplest truss is really a rafter system with ceiling joists connected to it. Since the ceiling joist is the lower chord, it is in tension and a steel rod can be substituted for it.

RAFTER SYSTEMS

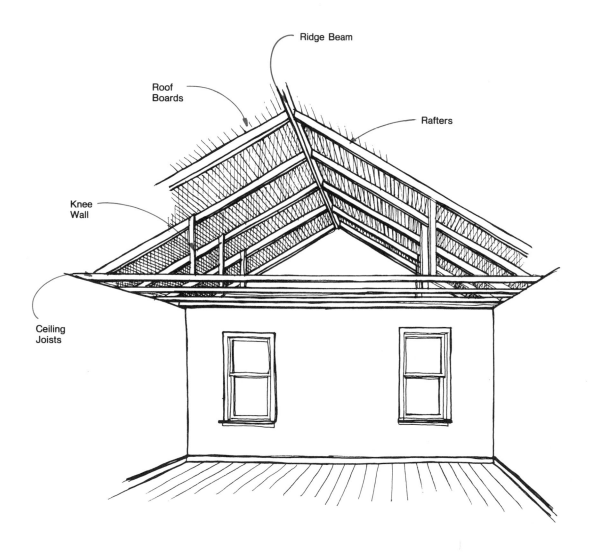

More complex trusses begin with the kingpost truss and have been developed into a large variety of complex assemblages capable of spanning long distances with the least material. The simplest and most commonly used truss is the bar joist. Bar joists are built with steel chords of double angles and webs of steel bars bent in accordion fashion. Available in a great range of depths and lengths, they are the most common commercial floor and roof structures.

In recent decades, adventuresome architects and engineers have developed some completely new structural systems. The most famous is Buckminster Fuller's geodesic dome, which is the epitome of the greatest span with the least amount of material. More common today is the "space frame," where simple trusses are interconnected to span at right angles, and even additionally on the diagonals. This creates two- and four-way truss systems. Thin-shell concrete has had its adherents; often it is used following geometric curves, such as the hyperbolic parabola, in order to build forms for three-dimensional curves with straight boards.

Air-support structures have become familiar as winter covers for pools and tennis courts; they have also been used for world's fair pavilions and stadiums. In these, an internal air-pressure rise of an unnoticeable amount becomes a respectable uplifting force. In recent years, interest in structural exploration has fallen from fashion. No doubt it will come around again.

TRUSSES AND BAR JOISTS

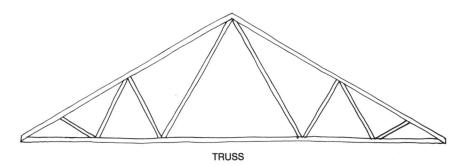

TRUSS

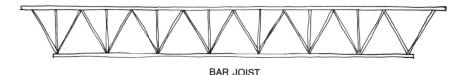

BAR JOIST

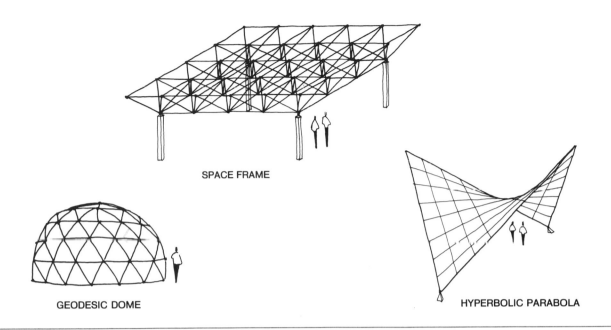

SPACE FRAME

GEODESIC DOME

HYPERBOLIC PARABOLA

Structure in Remodeling

Special problems in structure must be recognized in remodeling work. A change in occupancy may bring reduced live-load requirements that can permit more structural flexibility in a building than originally designed. Old mill buildings were sometimes designed to bear hundreds of pounds per square foot. Quite the opposite may be the case, too, requiring structural reinforcement for the new use.

Bearing walls can usually be penetrated without too much difficulty with the insertion of steel lintels. Caution must be exercised to determine which walls of an old building are bearing and which are not. Even more caution must be taken when considering removing columns and cutting holes in floors. In wood-and-steel structures this can usually be done, with proper compensatory work. Concrete structures, however, are far less tractable and require extremely careful analysis to determine if any alterations are possible.

In most cases, consultation with an architect or structural engineer will be required before a designer can propose structural changes.

Structure in Interior Design

The final paragraph above is of the greatest importance for interior designers. An understanding of basic structural principles is important for the practice of interior design, but it is dangerous—both actually and legally—to make structural alterations without consulting an architect or engineer. While the rare major mishap has occurred even with these consultants on the project, the responsibility in those cases is theirs.

The most common form of interior construction that designers must specify is interior partitions. Whether for loft buildings, high-rise buildings, or house renovations, the usual structural system for partitions is light framing: 2″ × 4″ (50 × 100 mm) metal or wood studs spaced 16″ (400 mm) on center. This system, which is derived from light wood framing systems in use since the middle of the nineteenth century, is still the most prevalent structural system in use in residential construction today. In commercial structures metal studs are more likely to be used than wood studs. There is relatively little difference in construction procedure. Since these partitions bear no weight other than their own, it is seldom necessary to call in a structural consultant. Removing or cutting holes in walls or floors is within the competence of an experienced builder. Where building codes are in place, the community building department will exercise control.

It is good practice for interior designers to understand the principles of wood-frame construction. Architectural woodwork, such as shelving and countertops, may not be engineered, but it is subject to the same stresses of bending forces as beams. In the case of furniture, structure is based upon conventions developed over years of practice. For example, from experience one knows that the most common thickness of lumber used for shelving, ¾″ (19 mm), can carry a satisfactory load over a span of about 3′ (90 cm). It is possible to hang units on walls, but chests and cabinets, whether freestanding or built-in, will be structurally and visually sounder if the uprights carry the weight to the floor surface.

The next most common structural concern for designers is ceilings. Suspended ceilings are often used to cover mechanical services distributed across the ceiling space. The new ceilings are hung by wires from the structure above, a process that is described more completely in the section on surfaces (see page 143).

Designers are frequently involved in the design of stairs. They are freestanding structures and must be capable of bearing heavier loads than most floors. The design must quite carefully conform to the code adopted by the building department having jurisdiction.

All designers must become accustomed to the necessity of conforming to codes. In addition to the building code, the life-safety, accessibility, and other codes must be reviewed for each project. These are forever changing, and it is essential to consult the latest edition.

2 Wood

Wood is a hard, fibrous material, mostly xylem, that forms the greater part of the trunks and limbs of trees. It is probably the oldest building material of all, at least in areas where trees grew. Wood is light in weight, high in tensile strength, and easy to work—all factors desirable for construction. In the earliest probable structural use by man, saplings were bent together at their tops, and their branches were interwoven, to create shelter. Later, poles were set in holes in the soil with crossmembers lashed to them. As better tools were developed, poles were squared into timbers and assembled, often with intricate joinery. The development of light wood frame construction awaited the invention of the power saw, cheap nails, and the plentiful forests of North America. The development of newer wood products, such as plywood and laminated timber, was stimulated by the enormous shortage of construction materials caused by World War II. Originally developed for boat construction, these wood products quickly found many other applications, even for aircraft structure. Various composition boards awaited the development of synthetic resins.

Properties of Woods and Lumber

There are two broad classifications of wood. That which comes from coniferous or evergreen trees is called "softwood"; that from broad-leaf, mostly deciduous trees is "hardwood." These are terms of broad classification only, for some "hardwoods" (for example, basswood) are softer that some "softwoods" (such as yellow pine). Still, these terms are an industry standard and usually hardwoods are harder than softwoods.

Hardwoods are generally characterized by darker colored heartwood, with notable exceptions such as maple, birch, and ash. With close, even grain, these woods are hard to work, but mill (take shape by tooling) very well. Hardwoods tend to be heavy and strong.

Once plentiful, great forests of hardwoods covered much of northeastern and upper midwestern North America. Clearing for agriculture and ruthless timbering has all but eliminated hardwoods as an available source of lumber. That which does become available is mostly reserved for veneer and furniture construction. Of domestic species, oak is used mostly for flooring, maple for butcher block items and gymnasium flooring. Small quantities of walnut, butternut, cherry, and other ornamental species are too expensive for uses other than for fine furniture, trim, and edging for veneer. Veneer (very thin slices of selected woods glued to plywood, composition board, or lumber backing) has become the most common use of fine hardwood. A good deal of hardwood has been imported in recent years, including lauan, teak, mahogany, rosewood, and more exotic species. At the present rate of exploitation, teak is nearly used up and the others will follow soon. It requires typically 150 years for hardwoods to reach timber size, so the foreseeable future can only bring higher cost and greater scarcity.

Softwoods are generally light in color, with the notable exceptions of cedar and redwood, and are open-grained with little apparent difference between heartwood and sapwood. Softwoods tend to be lighter in weight with greater resin content. The prognosis is not so gloomy for softwoods. Although the remaining primeval forests are dwindling rapidly, the relatively quick growth of coniferous trees assures a steady supply into the future. Indeed, southern yellow pine is being grown in farms even now, reaching timber size in thirty to forty years. Softwoods are the principal woods used for construction purposes; lesser grades and coarser varieties are used for structural lumber, finer grades for millwork and finish work.

The term "lumber" means wood sawn and dressed to standard size. Pieces 1¼" (32 mm) thick or less are called "boards," those from 1½" to 3½" (32 to 89 mm) are "dimension lumber." Greater thicknesses are called "timbers." The nominal size of lumber is the sawn size; the actual size is planed after seasoning. Thus a 2" × 4" board is actually 1½" × 3½". Larger sizes (8" [200 mm] or more) are reduced ¼" (6 mm) more. Because wood is naturally unstable, these dimensions may vary ⅛" (3 mm) or even more. The lengths are standardized in 2' (600 mm) increments. Stock sizes are up to 12" (11¼") × 20' (300 mm × 6 m). Greater widths and lengths are available on special order only, at premium prices.

LUMBER SIZING

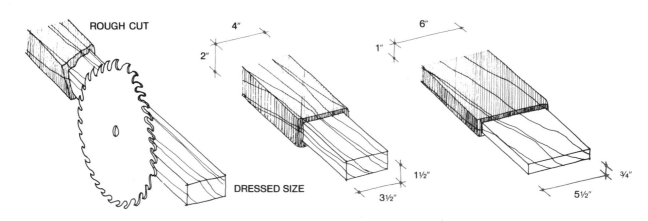

STANDARD SIZES OF BOARDS AND DIMENSIONAL LUMBER

NOMINAL SIZE	ACTUAL SIZE
Boards	
1 × 2 (25 × 51 mm)	¾ × 1½ (19 × 38 mm)
1 × 3 (25 × 76 mm)	¾ × 2½ (19 × 64 mm)
1 × 4 (25 × 102 mm)	¾ × 3½ (19 × 89 mm)
1 × 6 (25 × 152 mm)	¾ × 5½ (19 × 140 mm)
1 × 8 (25 × 203 mm)	¾ × 7¼ (19 × 184 mm)
1 × 10 (25 × 254 mm)	¾ × 9¼ (19 × 235 mm)
1 × 12 (25 × 305 mm)	¾ × 11¼ (19 × 286 mm)
5/4 × — (32 × — mm)	1 × — (25 × Widths same as ¾)
6/4 × — (38 × — mm)	1¼ × — (32 × as above)
Dimension Lumber	
2 × 2 (51 × 51 mm)	1½ × 1½ (38 × 38 mm)
2 × 3 (51 × 76 mm)	1½ × 2½ (38 × 64 mm)
2 × 4 (51 × 102 mm)	1½ × 3½ (38 × 89 mm)
2 × 6 (51 × 152 mm)	1½ × 5½ (38 × 140 mm)
2 × 8 (51 × 203 mm)	1½ × 7¼ (38 × 184 mm)
2 × 10 (51 × 254 mm)	1½ × 9¼ (38 × 235 mm)
2 × 12 (51 × 305 mm)	1½ × 11¼ (38 × 286 mm)
3 × — (76 × — mm)	2½ × — (64 × — mm same as 1½)
4 × — (102 × — mm)	3½ × — (89 × — mm as above)

Timbers

All wood members with both nominal dimensions exceeding 6″ (152 mm) may vary more in actual size, but will be about ¾″ (19mm) less than each nominal dimension.

Lumber is taken from living material and cannot be considered inert. When freshly cut, wood contains a high degree of moisture and is called "green." Green lumber is structurally weak and subject to shrinkage, splitting, and warping until it is dried or "seasoned." Seasoning may be accomplished by air drying, which takes one or more years, or kiln drying, which may take a matter of hours. Even after seasoning, wood must be expected to expand and contract, mostly across the grain, and to warp, because of moisture changes brought on by variations in humidity. While there are ways to control these changes, good design details must be utilized to minimize these effects and those due to differential expansion. The latter is a cause of warping that results from the assemblage of materials that do not expand and contract equally.

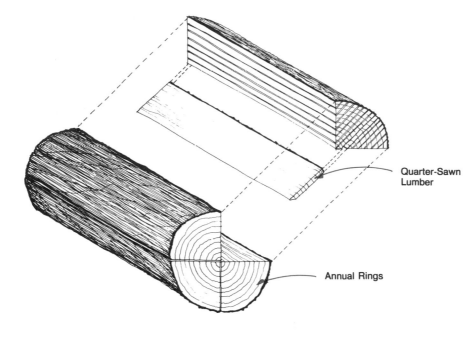

QUARTER-SAWN LUMBER

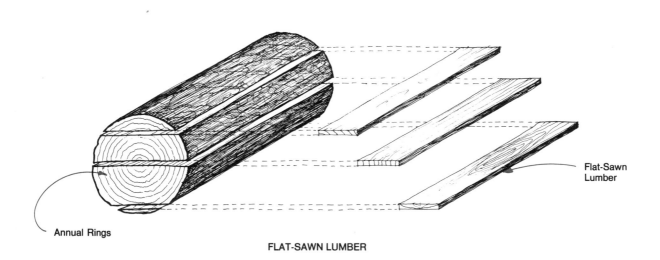

FLAT-SAWN LUMBER

The way the lumber is sawn from the tree makes a difference. When cut across the annual rings (quarter-sawn), wood is less subject to warpage than when cut tangentially (flat-sawn).

The great enemy of wood, aside from fire, is the disease we call decay. Despite the misnomer "dry rot," there is seldom decay in wood that is kept dry. Much design and detailing is developed to this end, including the various laps and overhangs. Good paint coating helps, as do various chemical treatments. Wood must be kept from contact with the soil, masonry, and concrete, which must always be assumed to be damp.

Certain woods, notably redwood, cedar, cypress, and teak, have high natural resistance to decay. Pressure treatment is very effective, but can only be done well with yellow pine, which is not usually suitable for finish work. Decay is a disease, and once wood is infected, the only treatment is the removal and replacement of the affected parts.

Termites are the other major enemy of wood, which is their food. A ground-nesting colony insect, termites are extremely destructive creatures. Sometimes called "white ants," termites were once confined to the South, but have been gradually appearing further north. Today only the most northern areas may still be free of them. In new construction, metal shields at the foundations and ground treatment are effective preventatives. Pressure-treated lumber is protected. In existing buildings, inspection and subsequent treatment, if warranted, are necessary. After the infestation is destroyed, damaged areas must be located and repaired.

Plywood. Plywood sheets are formed from thin layers of wood that are peeled from large logs and glued together under heat and pressure. Since the alternate layers are arranged with the grains at right angles, there is good resistance to splitting or tearing, even when nailed near the edge. The cross-grain assemblage also does much to reduce warping and increase dimensional stability. Sheets range in thickness from ⅛″ to 1¼″ (3 to 32 mm) thick, of three to seven or more plies. Standard sheet size is 4′ × 8′ (1.2 × 2.4 m). Greater lengths are available on special order at a premium price.

Plywood is graded according to the number of knots and other flaws per sheet. Inferior plies are used for interior layers, and the surfaces in these structural grades may be quite rough. Finish grades will be without these flaws (repairs may be evident) and will be sanded. The number of plies used usually increases with the thickness of the board. There is always an odd number of plies, so that both surfaces have the grain running in the same direction. The load capacity of the wood is greater when it is spanning in the direction of the grain. The larger number of plies is also a mark of quality; ½″ (13 mm) CDX (suitable only for rough sheathing) may have three plies, while fine quality Baltic birch plywood of the same thickness may have eleven. Most plywood is manufactured from softwood, commonly Douglas fir, and the grain is quite coarse. For a smoother finish, the surface plies may be one of several varieties of hardwood; this is called "paint grade." For casework, one or both outer plies may be of finer veneers of hardwood. This must be differentiated from "lumber core" veneer, where the veneer is applied to a core of edge-glued boards to simulate the characteristics of solid hardwood lumber for fine casework.

Plywood may be used for various surfaces, but it also has important structural qualities. Not only will it span joists and rafters to form rough floors or roofs, its resistance to splitting and tearing makes a membrane that can resist forces in all directions and that braces the structure diagonally. Plywood may also be used to build box beams and girders to create economical, lightweight structures. For sheathing purposes, plywood is available in a variety of milled textures, usually with vertical grooves at 4″ or 8″ (100 or 200 mm) spacing to simulate boards.

Composition Boards. Composition boards are wood by-products made from sawdust, chips, and shavings; bound together with resins, under heat and pressure, they form building boards of various types with many brand names. Most are nonstructural but have qualities that make them often more desirable than plywood. They are all cheaper than plywood and, being grainless, are subject to less warpage. They usually take paint finishes well and some may be attractive enough for natural finishes. The following are commonly available, but new types appear from time to time. Standard sheet size is 4′ × 8′ (1.2 × 2.4 m).

Hardboard, the generic term for the brand name Masonite, is perhaps the oldest particle board. Usually supplied in thicknesses of ⅛″ and ¼″ (3 and 6 mm), the surface is hard and smooth, sometimes with an embossed texture. Primarily a surfacing material, the board accepts adhesives well, but nails and screws are difficult to conceal.

Particle board is usually thicker and softer than hardboard. Composed primarily of sawdust, it ranges from ¼″ to ¾″ (6 to 19 mm) thick or more. While it may serve as a surfacing, it more often is used as an underlay for veneers or plastic laminates. Particle board is a heavy material, yet nonstructural. Because of its stability, it is frequently used for cabinets and inexpensive furniture.

Wafer board, with several brand names, is composed of large shavings and is considered a structural material suitable for roofing and sheathing; it is light in weight, and holds nails and screws well. The surface is heavily textured, and if this is acceptable, it may be naturally finished or painted.

Veneers. To be able to enjoy the color and grain pattern of increasingly rare hardwoods, the process of veneering was fully developed in the Renaissance and much used in the last century. Thin sheets ("flitches") of selected wood are glued, under pressure, to a cheaper base. These sheets are cut either by peeling a log as it is turned against a blade (rotary cut), or by slicing straight through the log (rift grain). Although traditional veneers are of substantial thickness, modern techniques pioneered by the Japanese produce veneers that are very thin—indeed, nearly two-dimensional. Today the usual backing for veneer is plywood or particle board, although in very fine work (architectural grade) the backing may be a core of edge-glued lumber. In every case, to avoid the warping due to differential expansion, the opposite surface must also be veneered. If not designed to be seen, this backing will be of inferior grade, even a different wood.

ROTARY-CUT AND RIFT-CUT PLYWOOD

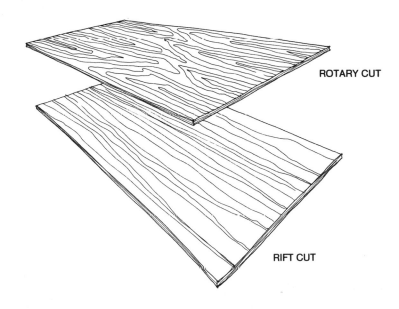

ROTARY CUT

RIFT CUT

EDGE TREATMENT OF VENEER

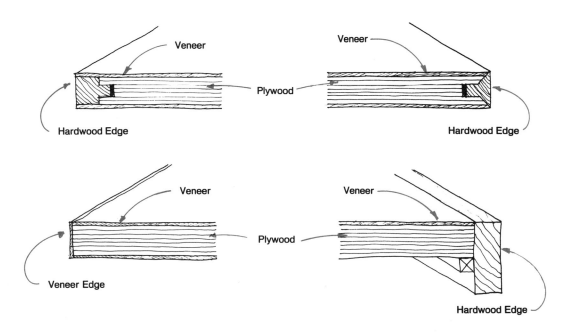

Veneer

Plywood

Hardwood Edge

Veneer

Plywood

Hardwood Edge

Veneer

Plywood

Veneer Edge

Veneer

Plywood

Hardwood Edge

In custom work, the flitches may be selected and numbered as they are sliced to maintain similar grain pattern. They may be alternately reversed (book matched) to intensify a grain pattern. Exotic graining from the burl (the trunk near the roots) or even diseased areas are often prized. The result may be finished in the same manner as solid wood; it gives much the same appearance.

The edge treatment of veneer requires special consideration. The edges may be veneered also, but they will be easily damaged. In finer work an edge strip of matching hardwood is glued flush to the piece, often making the perception of veneer difficult.

Wood Construction

The earliest type of wood construction, braced frame construction, consists of large timbers assembled as posts and beams with smaller members mortised into them for bracing.

These early timbers were originally hand hewn with axes; in later years they were hand sawn. The space between the posts was infilled with brick or with woven twigs (wattle) and plastered. The roof timbers had poles secured at closer intervals and were thatched; later roofs were shingled. This method of construction is typical "half timber" construction. The early New England settlers quickly found that this was inadequate protection from the severe winters there and covered the exterior walls with lapped boards (clapboards).

With a shortage of labor, the settlers devised water wheels to run their long saws in a reciprocating fashion. In the 1840s, large circular saw blades more directly translated the rotation of the mill to the blade. Machine manufacture of nails began at about the same time, followed by the development of light wood frame construction.

POST AND BEAM WITH MORTISED BRACE

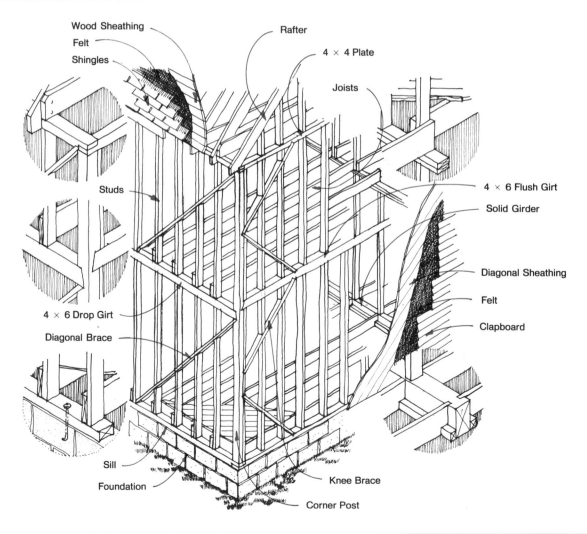

Wood Sheathing
Felt
Shingles
Rafter
4 × 4 Plate
Joists
Studs
4 × 6 Flush Girt
Solid Girder
Diagonal Sheathing
Felt
Clapboard
4 × 6 Drop Girt
Diagonal Brace
Sill
Foundation
Knee Brace
Corner Post

The earliest use of the more standardized lumber sizes in the 19th Century was to infill the braced frames and provide nailing for the sheathing. It became apparent that light members alone could provide structure. Because clapboards were split radially from 4' (1.2 m) logs, as were plaster laths, fractions of and multiples of 4' became the standard module for the new system. Thus 16" (400 mm) spacing of the vertical members, or studs, provided four nailing points for the clapboards and laths. The same spacing was just about right for the span of joists (flat spanning members) and rafters (sloping spanning members), with 1" (25 mm) boards for decking and roof sheathing.

A technique carried over from braced frame construction is the prefabrication of walls on the ground, which are later tilted up into position. When applied to light wood frame construction this is called balloon framing. This system has been used for buildings of up to five stories, although such structures are rare today. A "ribbon strip" (usually 1" × 4" [25 × 100 mm]) is secured to prepared cutouts in the studs ("let in") to support the joists. These are the characteristics of balloon frame

BALLOON FRAMING

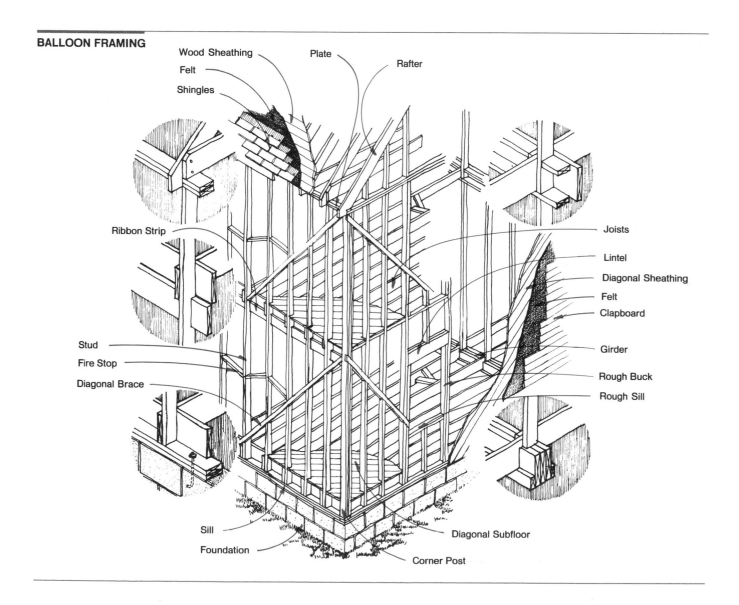

Wood Sheathing
Felt
Shingles
Plate
Rafter
Ribbon Strip
Stud
Fire Stop
Diagonal Brace
Sill
Foundation
Corner Post
Diagonal Subfloor
Joists
Lintel
Diagonal Sheathing
Felt
Clapboard
Girder
Rough Buck
Rough Sill

construction. Such buildings can be erected very quickly and, when properly braced and anchored, can withstand most natural disasters except fire. To slow flame spread through such an open frame, "fire stops" of wood blocking are inserted between the studs and joists.

In the middle of the nineteenth century, a different technique was developed, apparently in the West, called platform or Western frame. This construction method consists of first constructing the floor, including the rough decking, then assembling the walls, for that floor only, on the deck and tilting them up into position. These support the next floor joists and deck upon which the walls for the next floor are assembled and so on. This process has certain advantages, providing a level deck for working and manageable walls for a small crew. The disadvantage lies in the cumulative shrinkage through the joists and plates, which can be as great as ½" in 12" (13 mm in 300 mm). This is enough to cause damage to surfacing materials. In balloon frame construction, the studs extend continuously (perhaps spliced) from foundation to roof, and shrinkage is minimal. Nevertheless, most wood frame structures of one or two stories are platform frame.

Regardless of the system used, all light wood frame structures must be braced against wind, seismic movement, and other horizontal forces. Traditionally, this was done by letting in diagonal braces (usually 1" × 4" [25 × 100 mm]) at the corners. Another traditional system, used when rough sheathing was composed of 1" (25 mm) boards, was to secure this sheathing diagonally across the studs. Both systems create a triangular structure that is the basis for all bracing. Today plywood is the principal rough or even finish sheathing; its inherent membrane effect provides secure bracing.

While joists may be used for roof construction, more commonly rafters are used. Rafters have the advantage of leaning against each other, therefore spanning only half the distance needed for joists. The weakness of rafter construction is that it generates a good deal of side thrust, which must be countered in some way. The most common method is to tie the top wall plates together with ceiling joists, which absorb the thrust. This triangular structure is a simple truss. Trusses can be made more efficient by reducing the spans of the members with other members, creating more, and smaller, triangles. Because the connections at the joints must be very good, trusses are usually shop-fabricated and delivered to the building site ready to install.

Since large timbers have become scarce in the last fifty years and seasoning is difficult, lamination has been developed to fill the gap. Thanks to reliable and permanent adhesives, smaller pieces of lumber can be glued together to create large timbers. They can be formed, tapered, and bent to any configuration to suit the demands of structure and the designer. Higher quality lumber can be used on surfaces where both structure and appearance are most demanding. These are usually factory-fabricated and may be shipped to the site completely finished.

PLATFORM FRAMING

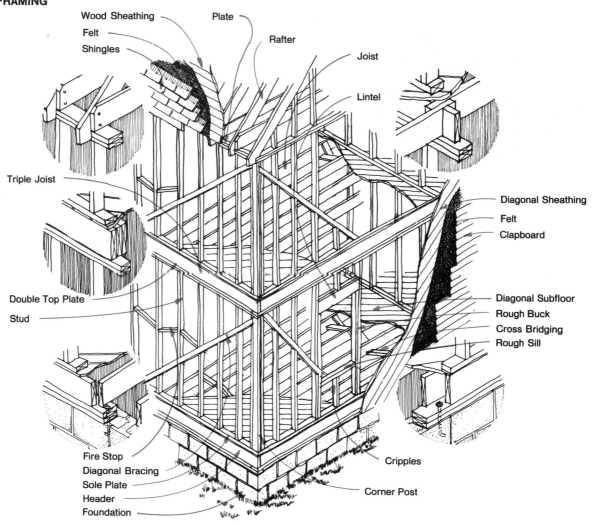

Wood Sheathing
Felt
Shingles
Plate
Rafter
Joist
Lintel
Triple Joist
Diagonal Sheathing
Felt
Clapboard
Double Top Plate
Stud
Diagonal Subfloor
Rough Buck
Cross Bridging
Rough Sill
Fire Stop
Diagonal Bracing
Sole Plate
Header
Foundation
Cripples
Corner Post

TRUSS DIAGRAMS

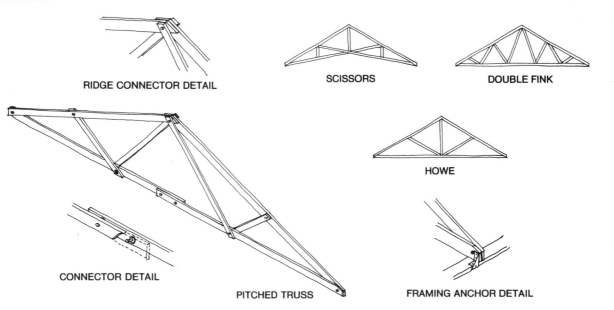

RIDGE CONNECTOR DETAIL

SCISSORS

DOUBLE FINK

HOWE

CONNECTOR DETAIL

PITCHED TRUSS

FRAMING ANCHOR DETAIL

Plywood and glue combine with lumber to form two types of structure developed in the late 1950s: box girders and stressed skin ("sandwich") panels. These unconventional structures place the most material where it counts. In the box girder, lumber is used at the top and bottom, where the stress is greatest; plywood sides hold the shape and resist the horizontal shear. Stressed skin panels utilize the sheathing as both structure and finish surface. Originally developed for aircraft construction where light weight is paramount, this system is now finding its way into the building industry.

These and other innovative construction systems have been made possible only through the development of modern organic adhesives. The systems are fascinating to designers, but they invariably cost more than conventional construction except where special considerations of weight and speed of construction are a major consideration. Perhaps as conventional materials become scarcer and costlier, the use of these efficient systems will become more widespread.

BOX GIRDER, LAMINATED BEAM, AND STRESSED SKIN PANEL

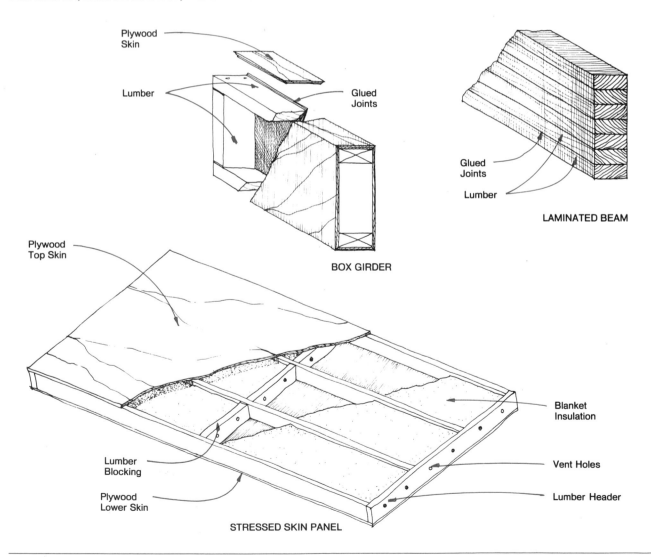

Plywood Skin

Lumber

Glued Joints

Glued Joints

Lumber

LAMINATED BEAM

BOX GIRDER

Plywood Top Skin

Blanket Insulation

Vent Holes

Lumber Blocking

Lumber Header

Plywood Lower Skin

STRESSED SKIN PANEL

FABRICATION OF CLAPBOARDS AND BEVEL SIDING

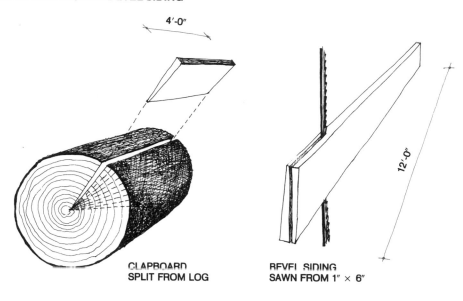

CLAPBOARD
SPLIT FROM LOG

BEVEL SIDING
SAWN FROM 1" × 6"

4'-0"

12'-0"

FABRICATION OF WOOD SIDING

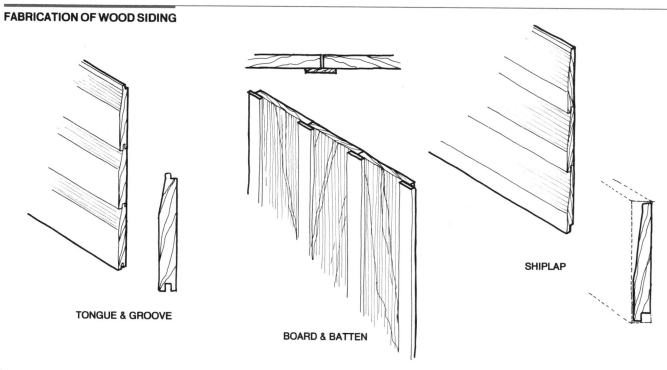

TONGUE & GROOVE

BOARD & BATTEN

SHIPLAP

As exterior sheathing, or interior wall finish, wood may be used basically as boards or plywood. The early clapboards are now resawn on the diagonal from 1" × 6" or 8" (25 × 150 or 200 mm), are 12' (3.7 m) or more long and are now properly called bevel siding.

Whatever the board treatment, the intent is to reduce wind and water penetration and to control warping and shrinkage. Over the years, a great many sheathings, or "sidings," have been developed to satisfy these requirements as well as the designer's fancy. Most are seen only in older buildings; however, tongue-and-groove, shiplap, and board-and-batten treatments are all commonly in use today.

The increasing use of plywood prevents many problems while creating new ones for the designer. Plywood sheets are large, but treatment of the exposed joints becomes a major design consideration. Various groove systems may conceal the side joints, but they do not conceal the end joints. Plywood's ability to cover large areas quickly and its innate bracing properties make it the material of choice for lower cost construction. Composition boards are also gaining in use, despite their generally inferior structural values. Often embossed with wood grain and installed to resemble bevel siding, they are characteristic of only the very lowest cost construction.

WOOD JOINTS

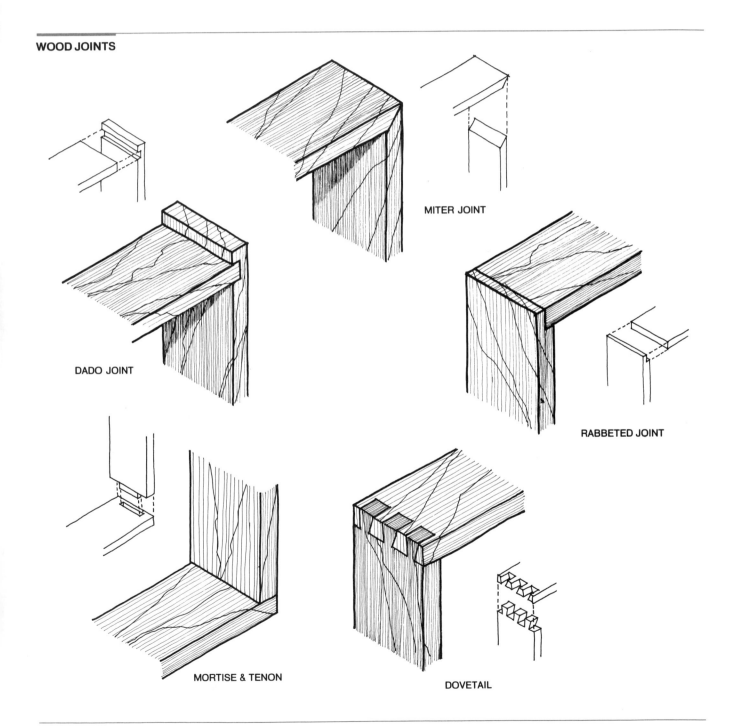

MITER JOINT

DADO JOINT

RABBETED JOINT

MORTISE & TENON

DOVETAIL

Shingles are small (16″ long × 4″ to 12″ wide [400 mm long × 100 to 300 mm wide]) pieces of wood sawn or split from cedar or, now rarely, cypress. They are laid in lapped rows as siding or roofing. If sawn, they are properly called shingles; if split, they are called shakes. On vertical surfaces they are usually laid with the bottom 8″ (200 mm) exposed ("to the weather") to assure two layers of thickness. Vertical joints are lapped by the second layer. On roofs (with a minimum slope of 4/12) shingles and shakes are laid to produce three layers.

Joinery. Over the ages elaborate systems for assembling wood, called joinery, have been developed. They mean to serve two purposes: to conceal edge grain (which is fragile and finishes darker than the rest) and to mechanically lock the pieces together, or at least increase the surface area for glue. While the development of modern cements has obviated most of the latter concern, the former is still with us.

While cabinetmakers may love joinery as a demonstration of skill and beauty, only a few of the traditional joints need concern the designer today. Such is the strength and reliability of today's adhesives that wood can be assembled much to the whim of the designer. Those joints that still have importance include the miter, the rabbet, the dovetail, the mortise and tenon, and the dado.

The miter, familiar in picture frames, conceals the end grain admirably but tends to be fragile. Many variations have been developed to attempt to correct this. The rabbet reduces the visible end grain, stabilizes the joint, and increases the glue area. The dado, which is especially useful for adjustable shelves but can also be fixed, locks the joint and provides direct bearing while concealing end grain entirely.

Wood in Interiors

Throughout history wood has been the single most popular material for a large variety of interior uses. A natural material, its endless diversity provides a great deal of visual interest: warmth, endless choice of pattern, texture, color. No two pieces are exactly alike. Wood appeals to those who covet a relationship with nature in an often cold and impersonal environment. Finally, wood is readily available (though less so than in the past), and can be easily worked and shaped for boundless applications.

Until the development of plastics, wood was the most common material used for furniture, often with fabrics and sometimes with metals. Many pieces surviving from ancient times attest to the durability and popularity of wooden furniture. Examples abound: solid, veneered, shaped and carved, laminated, steam bent, and molded. The history of the decorative arts is probably best understood through the study of wooden furniture, even though in the twentieth century plastics and metals have become major materials in this field.

As an interior construction material, wood, historically and now, is most commonly used for finish flooring and wall paneling. Paneling, or wainscoting, was traditionally of high-quality material with fine detailing and finish. More recently wood has been used primarily for luxurious corporate offices. The inexpensive paneling most commonly available is prescored, prefinished ¼″ (6 mm) plywood, which has unsatisfying details. It may even be hardboard with a photographic process surface.

Under the general heading of architectural woodwork, wood is used for stairs, railings, doors, windows, built-in storage, and trim.

Occasionally, ceilings have been handsomely paneled, but recent designers more often have used wood for the creation of lighting baffles and troffers at the ceiling. Applying wood in deep textures is a device for acoustical control; this control frequently makes wood the predominant material in concert halls and auditoriums.

Flooring is one place where solid hardwood is often used. In recent years, oak has been the most common, usually in the form of narrow 2¼″ (57 mm) boards. These are supplied in short random lengths in order to exclude knots. They are, therefore, tongue-and-grooved both at the edges and ends. Nails are concealed by being driven diagonally through the edges. Maple is often used, especially in gymnasium floors, because the close, even grain minimizes splinter formation. Rarer hardwoods, particularly pecan, walnut, and teak, are occasionally used, at much greater expense. Short lengths of hardwood may be laid in various patterns to create a parquet floor. More recently, smaller strips (about 1″ × 8″ × ⅜″ [25 × 200 × 10 mm]), often of rare woods, are laid in organic cements for a new type of parquet floor that is often prefinished with hard resins. These may be an excellent and durable floor finish; those fabricated from plywood are much less so.

Ornamental details may be easily carved or shaped in wood, as demonstrated by many historic interiors that used carvings, moldings, and turnings for the creation of rich and ornate spaces. Examples of later ornamental uses of wood in interiors may be found in the work of Alvar Aalto. Recent fashion has produced more examples of decorative uses, as exemplified by Michael Graves's work. Despite the attraction of wood, it has often been treated in ways that negate its inherent properties and appearance. With many finishes available for wood, it is difficult to say which will be appropriate in any given case. Traditionally, oiled or waxed finishes were preferred by designers, although recently high-gloss lacquer has become fashionable. Over the years, wood has been bleached, stained, pickled, gessoed, painted, gilded, and distressed. Clearly, there is no one appropriate finish.

There are probably more imitation wood-grain surfaces than all the variety of trees available; but whenever real wood is used, the chances are good that the interior will be successful.

3 Stone

Stone is a natural concretion of earthy or mineral matter. Rock is a geological term for stone in situ, while stone is rock removed from its bed for use. However, the words are often used interchangeably.

Stone competes with brick and wood for the claim of being the earliest building material. While the choice was largely dependent upon the availability of local materials, the wind shelters found on the French Riviera, dating back to around 300,000 B.C., make a strong case for the primacy of stone. Of course, the extreme durability of stone has preserved for us far more ancient monuments than those made of any other material.

It may be that the mysterious dolmen, scattered all over western Europe, represent the oldest extant architectural expression; they probably only were doorways to earth tombs that are now eroded away. Whenever the need was perceived for permanence, stone was substituted for the traditional material, often carved to resemble an earlier work built of less durable material. Examples of this include the mastaba tombs of ancient Egypt, which duplicate the form of reed houses, and the clear transition of the Greek temple from wood through terra-cotta sheathing to the ultimate stone edifice.

DOLMEN, MASTABA, ARCHAIC GREEK TEMPLE

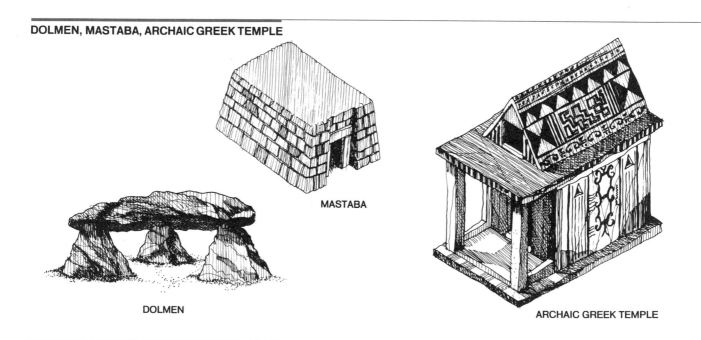

MASTABA

DOLMEN

ARCHAIC GREEK TEMPLE

We have a rich heritage of stone structures throughout the world—from the pyramids of Egypt to the neoclassical structures of the early twentieth century. Few are unmoved by the sight of the pyramids of Egypt and Central America, the classical temples, the great civil structures of Rome. Stone structure reached the peak of expression with the Gothic cathedrals of the twelfth century, which have not been surpassed. Stone is little used today as a structural material, but is still in much demand for sheathing, paving, and surfacing of every sort.

Properties of Stone and Marble

Stone is classified in three categories according to the method of formation: igneous, sedimentary, and metamorphic. Igneous stone includes all rock created directly from the molten state. This includes mantlerock as well as volcanic formations. It represents the core of mountain ranges and the slopes of volcanos. Originally liquid, igneous stone is solidified by the release of pressure and cooling, to become more or less crystalline in structure. Composed of many minerals in combination, these stones become coarse-grained if cooled slowly, finer-grained with more rapid cooling, and glassy with very rapid cooling. The igneous stones commonly used in building include granite, serpentine, greenstone, and basalt. They are typically very hard, strong, and resistant to chemical attack.

Granite is particularly durable and capable of taking a very high polish. It is available in shades from near white to black and almost any color or combination of colors. Vermont is the largest supplier of granite, but much comes from many other regions.

Serpentine is dense and polishes well, but not all types are suitable for exterior use. It ranges from olive green to greenish black, the darker shades having greater durability.

Greenstone is found principally in the Allegheny mountains of Pennsylvania. Heavy and close-grained, it ranges in color from pea green to moss green and darker. Greenstone is used mostly for paving, veneer, and landscape purposes.

Basalt is perhaps the most common igneous stone. Colored dark brown to black, it represents the black stripe of the characteristic churches of central Italy. It was a favorite of sculptors from as far back as early Egypt for its dark color and extreme hardness. Today that very hardness and its frequency of faults has limited its use, for the most part, to crushed stone.

Sedimentary rock is created in two ways: by the weathering away of primeval outcrops and the subsequent deposit of those silts and sands by wind or water; and from the precipitation over millennia of the remains of tiny calcium-bearing sea organisms, often mixed with larger shells and bones, on sea bottoms. Geological ages, heat, and pressure, along with chemical concretion, change the silts and calcium strata into rock. The former is generally referred to as sandstone, the latter as limestone. Both are typically deposited in layers, called strata. These stratifications vary greatly according to the circumstances at the time of deposition. Very often limestones show little or no stratification, while certain sandstones are most highly stratified and easily split along a stratum, or cleavage plane.

The sandstones commonly used for construction are called sandstone, conglomerate, and shale. Sandstones are mostly silicon, aluminum, and iron oxides, ranging from buff to dark brown in color. Occasionally sandstone may be blue or quite red, like the Longmeadow stone favored by H. H. Richardson for trim. Sandstones are sometimes mixed with pebbles: sandstones are called conglomerate or "pudding stone" if the pebbles are rounded, and "breccia" if the pebbles are broken. Shales are composed of fine-grained silt, often mixed with calcareous material; they vary greatly in hardness.

Limestones, in the purest state, are calcium carbonate: a white mineral commonly called "lime," which is only slightly soluble in water. Frequently the color is altered by the presence of other minerals, so that the natural color of limestone ranges from near white through grays to buff and brown. The most common limestones used for construction today include the oolithic, dolomitic, crystalline, and travertine. Limestone that is composed in part of small skeletal remains and which may contain a high percentage of shells and fragments is called oolithic. These shells are often clearly visible on cut surfaces. The most plentiful source of oolithic limestone in the United States is Indiana. Those limestones rich in magnesium carbonate and, consequently, somewhat crystalline in texture are called dolomitic. These are less hard but more easily worked than oolithic limestones. When composed almost purely of calcium carbonate crystals, limestone is called crystalline. This type of high-strength stone was used to build the great Gothic cathedrals.

A special case must be made for travertine, a limestone produced by the evaporation of water from hot springs. It has a characteristic texture created by small open pockets that appear in a horizontal, stratified manner. Much of Rome was built of travertine, and it became a great favorite of Mies van der Rohe and, consequently, the entire International Style. Travertine is often incorrectly called marble.

Sedimentary stone may further change over geological ages with heat, pressure, and mineral intrusions until it attains a harder, more completely crystalline structure. These metamorphic stones are usually visibly stratified and often display veining and coloration from the mineral intrusions into earlier cracks. There is no distinct point at which metamorphosis may be said to occur. Rather, there is a whole range of metamorphic stone, from ordinary sedimentary stone through the most completely changed stone. The building industry considers any limestone hard enough to polish to be marble. The most quarried metamorphic stones include marble, slate, schist, and quartzite.

Marble, from limestone, is highly crystalline, with an endless variety of color, intrusive patterns, and veining. Marble has long been the most popular stone for surfacing and ornamental use of every kind. Capable of being highly polished, marble is also popular in honed and split faces. The pattern of use for monumental buildings was set by the Athenians with the stone from Mount Pentelicus: pentelic marble. The seemingly inexhaustible Carrara district of Tuscany supplied Renaissance architects and sculptors with fine-grained white marble; the district still produces heavily today. In the United States, marble quarrying came late; the White House and Capitol in Washington were built of painted sandstone for the lack of a worked marble deposit. Now large amounts of fine-crystalled stone is quarried in Vermont, while Georgia is famous for the large-crystalled Cherokee marble. Both marbles range from nearly white through shades of grey. Other regions of the country produce marble of varied color, but a good deal of highly decorative material is imported from all over the world, especially Italy.

Slate is a very hard and finely grained foliate (highly stratified) stone metamorphosed from silty sandstone. While it may be finished in any manner, such as the finely ground face once used as chalkboards, slate is especially prized for a face cleft along a natural stratum. This slightly patterned surface represents a moment of fossilized time in a very ancient lake bottom; it is never exactly repeated. Most often dark gray, or silvery to nearly black, slate may also range in reds and greens, often used in combination.

Schist and quartzite, derived from sandstones crystallized with strong silicate cementation, are less frequently used today. Split into roughly rectangular faces, they are most often used for veneer and landscape purposes.

Finishing Processes. Quarrying for building stones consists of removing, by drilling, sawing, and splitting, large rectangular blocks of suitable material and transporting them to mills for finishing as surfacing, veneer, and trim.

Surfacing refers to stone used in large thin sheets as a final finish material. Finishing for surfacing material begins by gang-sawing the quarried blocks into sheets. This is done by specialized machines such as the shot saw and the diamond saw. The shot saw is a serrated blade that picks up hardened steel shot and draws it across the stone to do the actual cutting. This is suitable for softer material such as sandstone or limestone. For harder stone, like granite, or brittle stone, like some marble, a diamond saw is used. With this saw, a smoother wire picks up diamond particles to do the cutting. Both saws are cooled by constant water flow. The standard thickness for most surfacing is 1″ (25 mm); other thicknesses are used for other purposes. If a rough or textured surface is desired, these sawn surfaces may serve. The shot-sawn surface will show characteristic deep striations; the diamond sawn surface has a finer texture. When a smoother finish is desired, the sawn sheets are honed by carborundum disks to a smooth finish, usually on both sides, which may be the final finish. Ultimately the sheet may be polished on one side if the stone is suitable. After the honing process, the standard sheet thickness will be ⅞″ (22 mm).

Stone in Construction

The designer usually deals directly with the quarry representative on any project involving stone. The designer sends drawings to the representative, who prepares shop drawings for every piece and returns these to the designer for approval, along with samples of the current run of the quarry for color and finish. The shop drawings will show any required holes or fittings and will identify finishes on surfaces and edges. Plans and elevations may be included to show the size and location of each piece. When the quarry representative receives final approval of the shop drawings, the pieces are fabricated accordingly, then crated and shipped to the construction site.

Traditionally, on vertical surfaces these sheets were set in mortar, often with metal clamps in slots in the edges. On horizontal surfaces they would have been set on a layer of wet plaster to prevent points of pressure from cracking the brittle sheets. Today an organic cement is more commonly used to secure any surfacing, although care must be exercised in selecting those cements that will not cause stains to penetrate the stone, perhaps years later.

Stone flooring had in the past been set in mortar beds over the subflooring to allow for uneven thickness. Today the stone sheets or tiles are "gauged," that is, ground to a uniform thickness, so that they may be set in organic cement. This is now done even to slate and other natural cleft-face stone.

EDGE CLAMP DETAIL

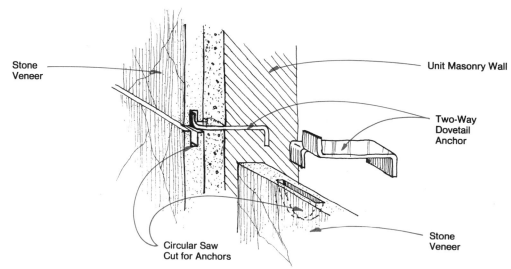

Stone Veneer

Circular Saw Cut for Anchors

Unit Masonry Wall

Two-Way Dovetail Anchor

Stone Veneer

Stone veneer refers to the use of a layer of stone as a wall surface. Smaller, thicker pieces of stone are applied to a wall to make it resemble a traditional, load-bearing stone wall. Thus veneer is a facing that may be applied to the real structural wall, whether it is wood, steel, or other masonry. In constructing a masonry veneer wall, the bottom course is set upon a shelf prepared in the foundation wall or a steel angle lintel. At regular intervals, metal ties secured to the backing wall are placed in mortar joints to tie the veneer to the structure. Steel angles may be used as lintels over openings, although true arches can be used at the discretion of the designer. Attention must be paid to proper flashing of exterior walls to prevent the penetration of water to the interior.

STONE VENEER ON WOOD FRAME AND UNIT MASONRY

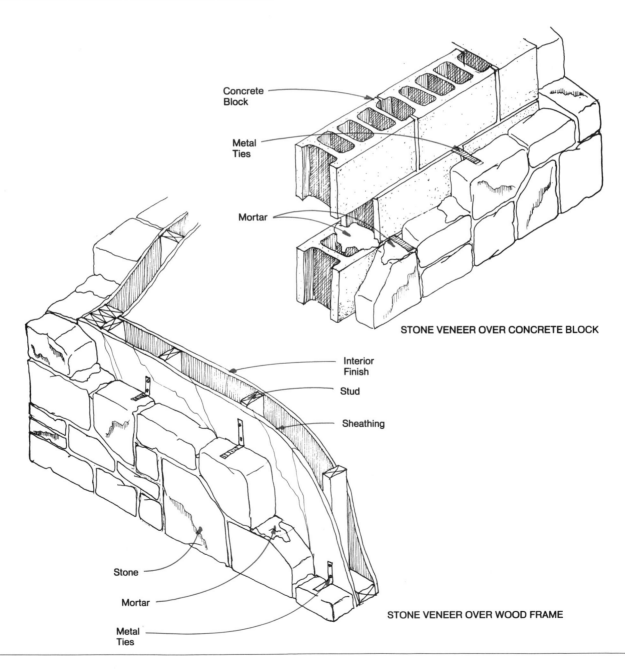

Concrete Block

Metal Ties

Mortar

STONE VENEER OVER CONCRETE BLOCK

Interior Finish

Stud

Sheathing

Stone

Mortar

Metal Ties

STONE VENEER OVER WOOD FRAME

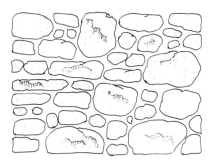

UNCOURSED RUBBLE

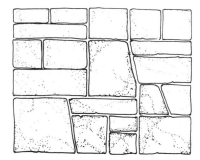

BROKEN ASHLAR

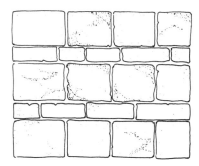

REGULAR COURSED ASHLAR

Stone wall facings are classified according to the shape of the stones and the pattern in which they are laid. The general types are fieldstone, rubble, and ashlar.

Fieldstone is rounded stone left by receding glaciers and used as found. These stones make a very thick wall and, because of their roundness, require so much mortar that little stone can be seen on the wall surface.

Rubble is quarry-run stone of various sizes and shapes, although rough rectangularity may predominate. Rubble may be uncoursed or coursed. Coursing means that at certain points in the wall a horizontal mortar line develops. The mortar joints will be irregular in thickness.

Ashlar walls are built of stone that is sawn or dressed to rectangular shapes, allowing the mortar joints to be of uniform thickness. All of the stones may be the same size, which produces a very uniform wall. The stones may also vary in size and be laid in an uncoursed or coursed manner. The faces may be any finish from quarry to honed or even polished.

Finishes. If the face of the stone is left as quarried it is called quarry face. A great variety of machine or hand finishes is possible. If the edges are cut back near the mortar joints so that the faces project, the stonework is called rusticated. Among machine finishes, in order of coarse to finer

POINTED FINISH

BUSH-HAMMERED FINISH

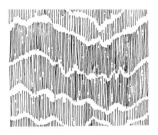

PEAN-HAMMERED FINISH

DROVE OR BOASTED FINISH

TOOTH CHISEL FINISH

CRANDALLED FINISH

texture are sawn (shot or diamond), milled, honed, and polished (the last really only suited to granite and marble). Hand finishes (assisted pneumatically today) produce variously hammered and chiseled faces, each carrying a distinctive finish. Hammered surfaces include bush, pean, pick, and crandalled. Chiseled surfaces include pointed, drove, and tooth-chiseled finishes.

In addition to surfacing and veneers, stone may also be used as trim in brick or stucco walls. The most common trims include arches, lintels, sills, and quoins. Trim is usually of ashlar, even in rubble construction. Arches permit the span of openings with small wedge-shaped stones. These cannot slip out of place unless the opening spreads. The sides of the opening at the springing of the arch must be well buttressed to resist this spreading thrust. As with brick, there are the three basic arches: semicircular (or Roman), segmental, and flat (or jack).

The semicircular arch has a radius equal to half the span. The segmental arch has a radius greater than that of the semicircular arch, and the flat arch, as the name implies, has no radius at all, although a slight rise (or camber) may be built in to correct the optical illusion of sagging. In any arch the center or keystone may be emphasized for its symbolic value.

In contemporary construction, a steel lintel is likely to be used, especially with a flat arch.

ARCH WITH NOMENCLATURE

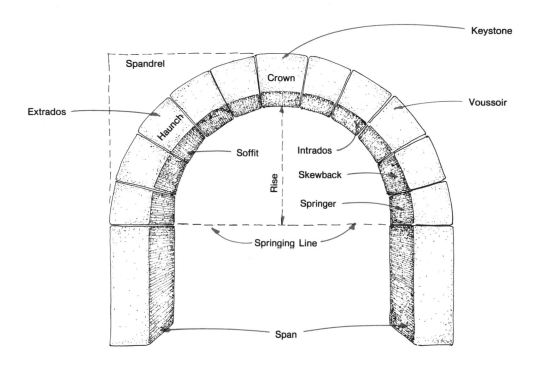

STONE ARCHES

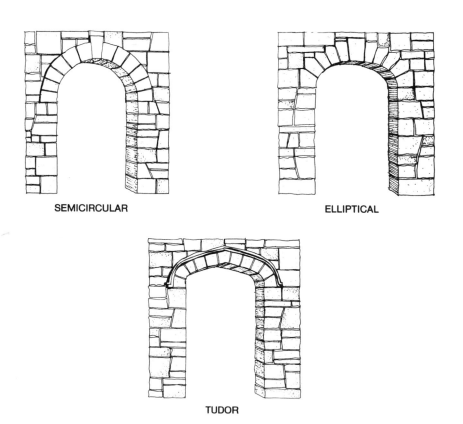

SEMICIRCULAR

ELLIPTICAL

TUDOR

CORBELED ARCH AND SILL

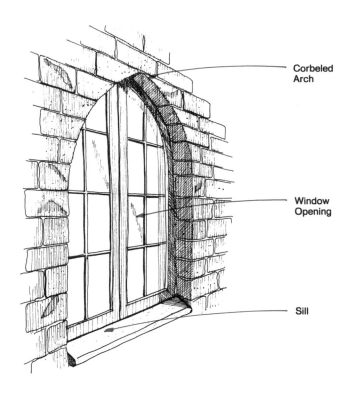

Corbeled
Arch

Window
Opening

Sill

QUOINS

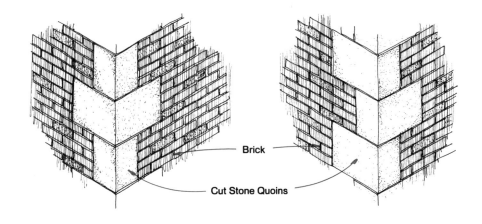

Brick

Cut Stone Quoins

BEAD AND VEE JOINT IN RUBBLE

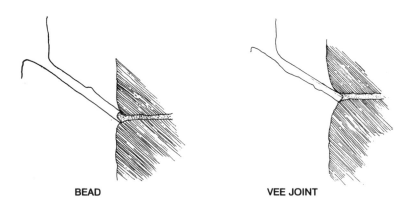

BEAD

VEE JOINT

A stone lintel is created by the use of a single large stone spanning the opening. The actual load on this lintel is not as great as it may seem because of the corbeled-arch effect created by the stone or brick above. Sills are carved from a single stone to extend across the entire opening. They are shaped with a wash to drain water to drip clear of a wall below.

Quoins are designed to emphasize the corners of a building, the part most vulnerable to abuse. They are usually of larger stones than the rest of the walls, they are often rusticated, and they have alternating wider and narrower courses that key into the walls.

Joints. The joints in stone surfacing are relatively few, and mortar is now seldom used to fill them. Today it is more likely that an organic sealant will be used. As with setting compounds, precautions must be taken to ensure that the sealant will not stain the stone. For setting stone veneer and trim, the same cement-lime-aggregate mixture used for brick is satisfactory; often a small amount of gypsum is added to reduce shrinkage. The natural gray color may be satisfactory, but white cement and selected light aggregate can be used when a lighter shade is desired. Mineral pigments are added when color is desired.

For ashlar, the same tooled joints are used as for brick, for the same reasons. For rubble it is common to present a neater finish by having a tooled mortar joint of a uniform thickness regardless of the actual width of the mortar itself. For this purpose a bead or vee joint is used.

When stone is used as an exterior material, care must be taken to select types that can withstand the local climate. Although a symbol of immutability, stone does weather—a process greatly accelerated in recent times. Freeze-thaw cycles of severe climates will cause spalling, the flaking off of the surface of more porous stones. Sandstone and some limestone may suffer this effect. Water penetrates the surface, freezes, and expands, forming cracks which amplify the process. Treatment with waterproofing compounds will help alleviate this problem.

In an age of industrial and automotive pollution, stone can be severely affected: from soiling and discoloration to actual melting away under the impact of acid atmosphere and rain. It is said that the great architecture and sculpture of Venice has degenerated more in the last few decades than in all the centuries before, principally from industrial pollution. Affected the most are limestone and marble; their basal chemistry neutralizes the acid, but in the process the stone surface is converted to salts that wash away. If limestone or marble exists in a project or is desired by the designer, regular treatment with waterproofing compounds will improve resistance to this degeneration. The stones that are most resistant to weathering and pollution are slates and granites. A visit to an old cemetery will be most revealing. Granite and slate monuments, although centuries old, will look as though they were carved yesterday. Those made of marble or limestone will look like sugar cubes melting away.

In renovation work some old stonework, such as granite, which shows little aging, may possibly be matched, especially if stone from the original quarry is still available. Stone from other locations in the building can be successfully moved, provided the entire stonework is ultimately cleaned. In most cases, the best direction for the designer is to use a harmonious but different material, since a bad match cannot be concealed.

Stone and Marble in Interiors

There are few uses for stone as a structural material for specifically interior application. The exception is fireplaces, including the chimney, which is often built of rubble. Frank Lloyd Wright was famous for his fireplaces, as was Marcel Breuer. The next most common use of stone is for flooring, although care must be taken to maintain level when changing flooring material. This has been made much easier with the introduction of gauged material, which may be only ⅜" (10 mm) thick.

Perhaps the most popular stone through the ages has been travertine. Many interiors have floors or steps of travertine that have been in continuous use for hundreds of years. Travertine will show wear; but even with floors and steps worn from abrasion, the material ages gracefully.

From the time when it was the typical palace flooring to the present, marble has always denoted exceptional interiors, or at least expensive ones. It may come as a surprise that compared with high-quality carpeting, or even vinyl tile, marble is not really more costly.

The problem of the thickness of stone may cause difficulty in renovations. Care must be taken when the subfloor is wood because deflection may crack the brittle tiles. A certain overdesign of structure may be necessary to minimize this problem. In public buildings the use of heavier stone set in a mortar bed over a masonry or concrete slab is still common practice to permit slope for drainage.

Stone floors can be used to create interesting patterns and elaborate designs. Examples of this use can be found in such civic buildings as the United States Capitol and other monuments. The permanence, ease of maintenance, elegance, and appearance of luxury make it surprising that stone floors are not used more frequently.

The stone surfacing of walls is generally restricted to large public spaces. Stone in a small space may feel heavy and cold, and can cause unpleasant acoustics. From the last century through the thirties, marble wainscoting was often used in commercial and public hallways, and until the fifties, marble banks were de rigueur. Recently, the most frequent use of stone and marble is in office-building lobbies and large civic structures. The common use of several different kinds of marble in one space, however, is considered bad taste, and even in large spaces an excess of stone can create a cold and forbidding experience. There are no formulas, however, for the proper use or amount of stone. Recently, travertine has become the material of fashion for modern office-building plazas and lobby spaces; outdoor paving and furniture; and indoor walls, paving, and furniture.

Marble has been an appropriate material for many years for such applications as tops on chests, lavabos, and sideboards. Although different varieties have varying resistance to staining, marble is unharmed by water and stands up better than most materials with less maintenance. Countertops, table surfaces, and consoles are equally suitable in marble and other types of stone. Slate also makes an excellent top and, if the budget permits, granite has no peer. As with flooring, it is possible to create beautiful surface patterns through the use of various stones. This was more popular in the eighteenth century; some lovely pieces of elaborate inlaid tops from that time have survived.

With its poor tensile strength, stone requires a substructure to support horizontal surfaces. Solid wood frames, many times with plywood bearing surfaces, are most often used. Occasionally sheets of stone can be used for furniture beyond horizontal surfaces. Some manufacturers have made quite beautiful cubes of marble and travertine for use as end tables or individual coffee tables. In addition, stone has always been a popular material for mantelpieces, thresholds, window sills, and other surfaces where permanence and ease of maintenance are important.

4 Brick

Brick is a modular ceramic building block, probably the earliest building material of urbanized societies. It is reasonable to expect that the stoneless alluvial plains of Mesopotamia would foster brick construction, but even in Egypt, where stone is everywhere, brick was used in the earliest tombs, or mastabas. These were of sun-baked brick. Certainly it is more convenient to use the material at one's feet than to cut it from the hills, especially with stone tools. As early as the seventh century B.C. the Ishtar Gate of Babylon was faced with fired glazed brick, although the core was sun-dried material. Fired brick largely built the Roman Empire, thereby denuding the forests of the Mediterranean for the necessary charcoal. Through the ages the use of brick has changed little, except that the fuel for firing became coal, and, later, natural gas.

Properties of Brick

It is sufficient to know the inherent properties and the parts of the process of manufacture that affect the final appearance of the product: color of the clay, method of forming the brick, temperature of the firing, brick size, and the bond or pattern used when the brick is laid, and the mortar used.

Color. Natural clays and shales quarried for brick manufacture range in color from nearly white through buff, salmon, various shades of red, to nearly blue. These clays are close to the color of the finished product except for some darkening when fired. With glazes, of course, color may be further modified. Grog (bits of fired ceramic) may be added to change texture and color and to reduce shrinkage. Iron filings are sometimes added to generate a speckled texture.

Molding Process. To the sifted clay, various amounts of water are added according to the molding process to be used: soft mud, stiff mud, or dry press. Each of these produce brick of quite distinctive appearance.

Brick molded using the soft mud process is also called wood-molded or, less accurately, hand-molded brick. A battery of wood molds is packed with soft mud, the excess of which is scraped from the top, after which the mud is turned out immediately. To facilitate the unmolding, the molds are either wet, which produces water-struck brick, or dusted with sand, which produces sand-struck brick. The sides of these bricks slope slightly inward toward the bottom, which usually has a depression or "frog," also containing the manufacturer's mark. This makes the brick easier to pick up and forms a key for the mortar. The top will have a scraped appearance from removing the excess clay. The sides of water-struck brick will have a smeared texture, while sand-struck brick will have a surface layer of fine sand never quite matching the color of the clay beneath.

The stiff mud process is one of extrusion in a continuous bar the length and width of the brick. This bar is wire cut to the thickness of the brick. Extruded brick is more precisely formed than wood-molded brick, except for the top and bottom where the wire cutting results in a "pulled" appearance. These surfaces will be concealed in a wall. It is characteristic of extruded brick to have a number of holes from top to bottom to make the drying and firing process more even; these also form keys for mortar.

The dry press process involves filling steel forms with a nearly dry clay mixture and packing them tightly with a hydraulic press. Not surprisingly, these are the most precise bricks of all—square, smooth, and uniform. Pressed brick may also have vent holes top to bottom.

TYPES OF BRICK MOLDING PROCESS

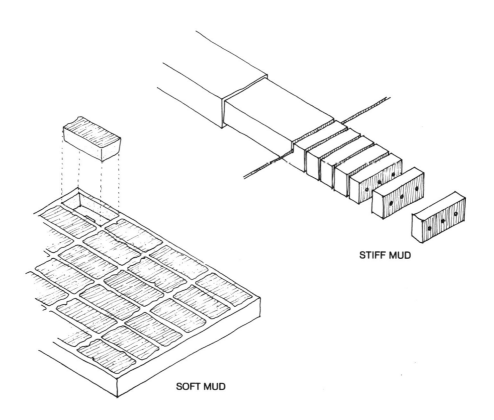

STIFF MUD

SOFT MUD

Firing. The dried bricks are stacked lattice-fashion in a kiln and fired to a high temperature. This temperature, however, is never uniform throughout the kiln. Temperature differences will result in color variance in every batch, despite the most stringent care. In general, the higher the temperature the darker the color the brick will be. Color variance is a brick characteristic, but may be exaggerated by "flashing," a process that emphasizes color variance. Some of the bricks in every batch will be scorched very dark and often warped and distorted in shape. These are called "clinkers" and were traditionally discarded or ground into grog. Now they are often prized and used to add texture to a wall.

Glazed bricks can be produced by a single firing. A chemical salt is introduced into the kiln, which gives to the brick a glossy and darker surface. True ceramic glazes may be painted on one or more surfaces before a second firing. These are decorative, impervious, and expensive.

Size. The term "common" has two connotations in brick terminology. Traditionally, common brick referred to the lower grade brick used on the interior of thick walls, as opposed to "face" brick, which is selected for the surfaces. Today the term usually means of "common" size: 3⅝″ × 7⅝″ × 2¼″ (92 × 194 × 57 mm). This is the modern "modular" size designed for the 8″ (200 mm) module that has become a building industry standard. This brick, along with the ⅜″ (10 mm) mortar joint, fits the module in length, with two wythes in width and three courses high. In buildings built prior to the middle of the twentieth century, common brick will be found to be 3¾″ × 8″ × 2¼″ (95 × 200 × 57 mm). Taking into account the mortar joint, these will not fit the 8″ (200 mm) module in length.

There are other sizes of brick available at the option of the designer. "Roman" brick, 1⅝″ × 3⅝″ × 11⅝″ (41 × 92 × 295 mm), a favorite of Frank Lloyd Wright, gives strong horizontal emphasis to a wall. To reduce warping during firing, these are usually extruded lengthwise as a cluster of four. Split apart, they have one smooth and one rough face to choose from. "Norman" bricks are the thickness of common brick, but the length of Roman brick, thereby giving less horizontal emphasis. Many other brick sizes have been introduced, usually in an attempt to be more economical in labor, without much success.

Bond. The term "bond" may refer to the adhesion of mortar to the bricks. But it may also mean the method by which a brick wall of more than one wythe is unified, so that these walls are not merely 4″ (100 mm) walls stacked next to each other. Today this may be done with metal ties or joint-reinforcement grids, but traditionally bond was formed by laying some brick as headers, thereby extending through two wythes. The necessity for bond courses developed the distinctive patterns of stretchers and headers that have been named.

TYPES OF BRICK

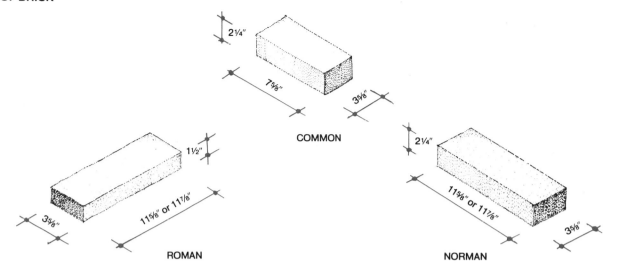

COMMON

2¼"

7⅝"

3⅝"

ROMAN

1½"

3⅝"

11⅝" or 11⅞"

NORMAN

2¼"

11⅝" or 11⅞"

3⅝"

BRICK POSITION TERMS

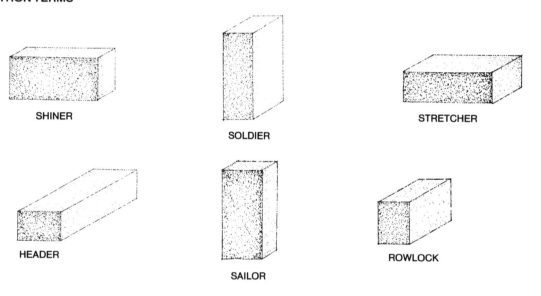

SHINER

SOLDIER

STRETCHER

HEADER

SAILOR

ROWLOCK

BRICKS IN POSITION

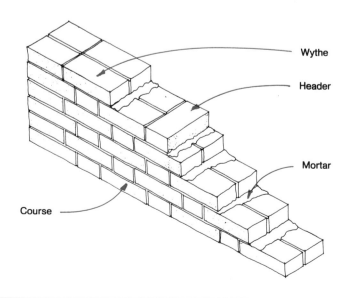

Wythe

Header

Mortar

Course

COMMON

STACKED

FLEMISH

RUNNING

ENGLISH CROSS

ENGLISH

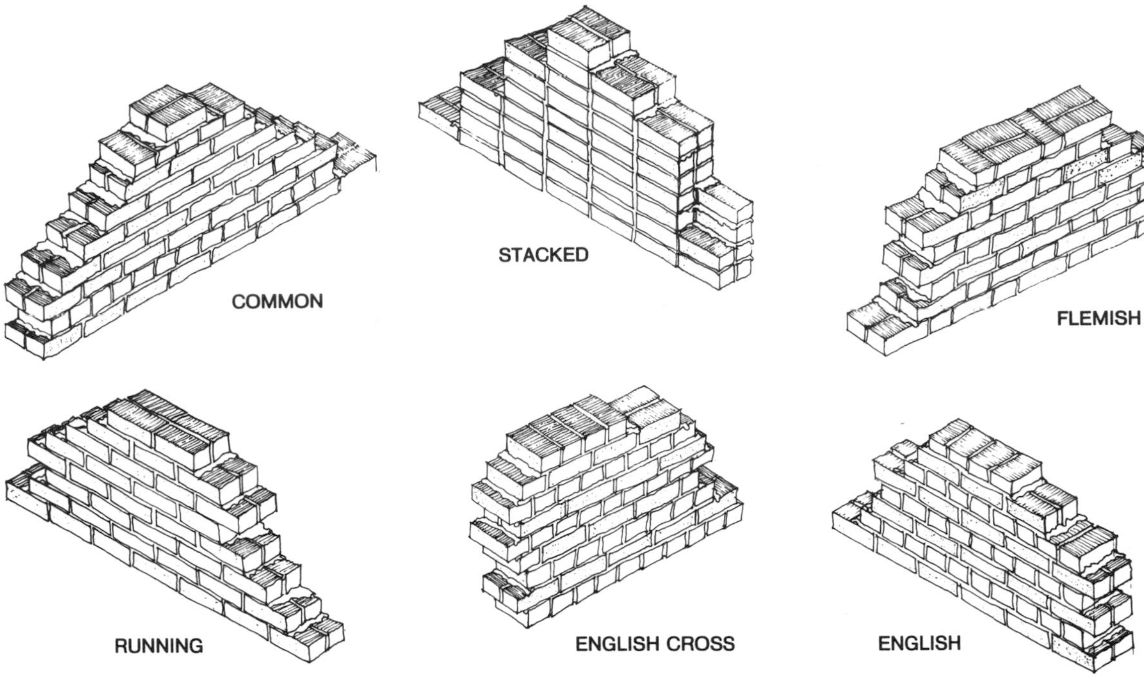

It should be noted that running and stack bonds are not bonds in the true sense, since these bonds do not extend beyond the face wythe; however, all brick wall patterns are referred to as bonds even when they are nonstructural. These latter two are often indicative of brick veneer construction, although not a completely reliable indication considering the use of metal ties for bond in some structural walls and the use of batts to form bond patterns in some veneer walls.

Mortar. Individual bricks are set in a paste called mortar, composed of a mixture of portland cement, fine aggregate (sand), lime, and water. Where structural soundness is a factor, the quality of the mortar becomes important; it is the weakest part of a brick wall. Since proportions and quality of ingredients, method of mixing, and the elapsed time between mixing and use are vital to the strength and adhesiveness of mortar, the designer, as is so often the case, must rely upon the skill and integrity of the mason for quality control. The color of the mortar may have a major effect upon the appearance of the finished wall or paving. Normal mortar is gray, either lighter or darker according to the aggregate used. White mortar may be obtained through the use of white portland cement and selected light aggregate. Pigments can be added to provide a wide range of colors, including black.

The type of mortar joint also affects the finished appearance. Any joint can be used on the interior, but tooled joints that compact the mortar and leave no shelf to collect water improve the resistance of an exterior wall to water penetration.

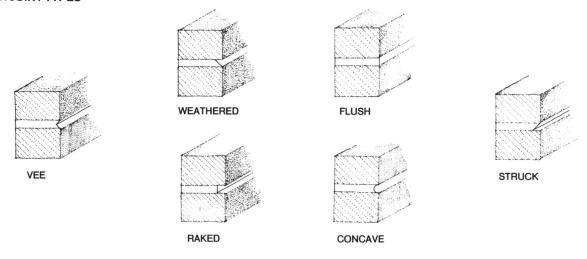

VEE

WEATHERED

FLUSH

STRUCK

RAKED

CONCAVE

Brick in Construction

Brick may be utilized as load-bearing structural walls or as veneer, which is a surface finish over another structure. Load-bearing walls may range from 8″ to 36″ (200 to 900 mm) or more, in increments of 4″ (100 mm), according to the height of the wall and/or loads to be borne. The bricks are laid in mortar and the joints completely filled, right from the foundation up. All necessary hardware, plumbing, and electrical conduits and boxes are installed as the work progresses. Openings are

ARCHES AND LINTELS

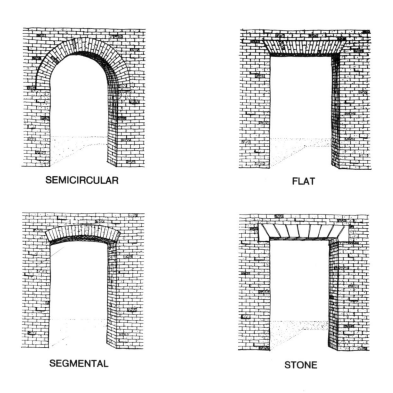

SEMICIRCULAR

FLAT

SEGMENTAL

STONE

spanned by arches or lintels. Buttresses may be built between the openings to stiffen a tall wall or carry a heavy loading condition.

True arch construction requires the brick to be "rubbed" (now more likely ground) to the proper wedge shape, while the mortar joint maintains uniform thickness. Today one often sees whole bricks used with wedge-shaped mortar joints.

Because a brick wall is not very watertight (particularly the mortar joints), a barrier in the form of a thin sheet of impervious material is often introduced to control water penetration. This material, called flashing, is traditionally copper, but may be other metals or even bituminous felt. Often extending through the wall, weepholes should be formed just above the flashing to drain the collected moisture.

Brick veneer may refer to a surface layer of brick over another type of masonry, usually concrete block, as backing. But often brick veneer means a nonstructural surfacing applied to a frame structure of wood or steel studs. In this case the brick rests directly upon a shelf prepared in the foundation wall, or shelves of steel angles fastened to the real structure. Metal ties secured to the understructure are set in the mortar joints to brace the single wythe. Outwardly, there may be few clues to reveal the fact that the wall is a veneer rather than a structural brick wall.

THROUGH-WALL FLASHING AND WEEP HOLE

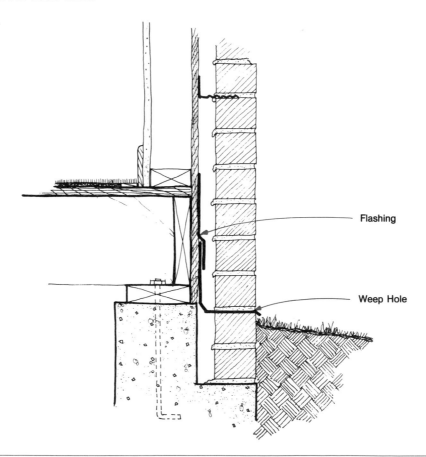

Flashing

Weep Hole

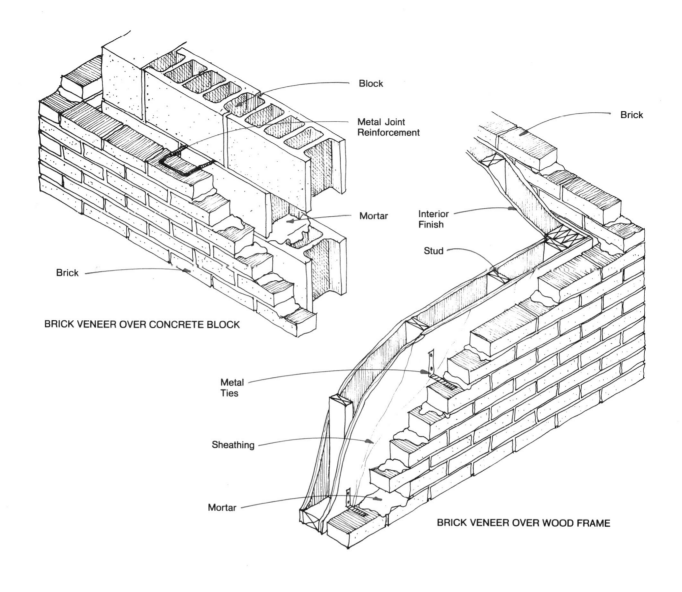

Block

Metal Joint
Reinforcement

Mortar

Brick

Interior
Finish

Stud

Brick

BRICK VENEER OVER CONCRETE BLOCK

Metal
Ties

Sheathing

Mortar

BRICK VENEER OVER WOOD FRAME

Brick Selection. When selecting brick, the designer must take into account the use to which the brick is to be put. Extruded brick, for instance, may not be considered suitable for paving because of the usual holes in the top. Dry-press bricks, on the other hand, may be too smooth. For paving, soft mud brick will present a solid top with enough "tooth" to prevent slipping. These same bricks in a wall will present a somewhat irregular appearance, while extruded brick will be much more regular and dry pressed brick will be even more precise and regular. It is not surprising that many designers prefer soft mud brick despite the higher cost.

After the designer specifies a particular brick, the supplier sends samples to the design office. Usually these samples include at least two bricks, one the lightest, the other the darkest in the color range. Several other shades may also be included. If the samples are approved, the supplier will reserve enough bricks for the particular job. For a large project it may be necessary to mix together several batches. If enough bricks are not reserved, no one can guarantee a color match. When the actual wall or paving is laid, the designer must rely upon the mason to utilize the bricks by random selection so that no discernable pattern appears (unless it is desired by the designer). To be certain that all concerned agree on the final appearance of the masonry, it is customary to build a sample wall or paving for the approval of the designer. After approval the sample wall becomes the model for all the workers on the site.

Cleaning and Sealing. While the mortar is still fresh, the brick may be cleaned by scrubbing with water. After the mortar hardens, projections can be removed by rubbing with a carborundum block. When the mortar is dry, a fine bloom of cement may appear over the brick. This can be cleaned by a 10 percent solution of muriatic acid, which will dissolve the mortar traces without attacking the brick.

To improve the water resistance of the wall, one or more coats of a silicone sealant may be applied. This seals the pores, while having little effect upon the finish appearance.

Adaptive Reuse. Designers will often have to deal with brick in the adaptive reuse of older structures. There is no way that new brick can be expected to match old brick. For certain limited applications, brick removed elsewhere from the building may be cleaned, and if great skill is exercised, be reasonably expected to match closely the existing wall if the entire building is cleaned. Light work may be accomplished with strong detergent solutions, while heavier cleaning may require acid or even sandblasting. The ever-vulnerable mortar joints will probably need to be raked and tuck-pointed, a process in which fresh mortar is applied with narrow irons and appropriately tooled and cleaned. Major additions or alterations are best done with some material that does not attempt to match the existing brickwork.

Brick in Interiors

Because brick is a natural material with desirable texture, it is popular among interior designers, although it must be primarily viewed as a structural rather than as a decorative material. Its inherent weight makes it inappropriate for many applications. Unlike most decorative surfacing materials, brick needs a proper foundation to carry its weight. It is also a material of some thickness and hence cannot arbitrarily be used as a surfacing or flooring. However, when interior designers work with architects at the inception of a new building or renovation, it may be possible to specify brick walls or floors for the sake of their appearance.

Brick is such a common material in older buildings, such as mills, town houses, and loft buildings, that designers must frequently deal with stripping and cleaning existing brick. The rough texture created by old brick is so often considered particularly desirable that an "old look" is frequently faked. This is a practice to be discouraged, since it is never very convincing.

There are certain appropriate settings for the use of brick, which relate to the nature of the material. Because of its weight, brick is seldom used for partitions or wall surfacing in high-rise buildings. Therefore the introduction of brick planters or brick walls in buildings not designed for brick rings a false note and may look out of place. When brick is simulated with some other material (such as vinyl or wallpaper), the result is affected, appropriate in a stage set but not in a real building. The use of brick as flooring is surprisingly rare, mainly because its thickness must be accommodated from the beginning. Nevertheless, sealed and waxed brick floors are among the most serviceable and attractive of flooring surfaces.

No matter what real or sentimental preferences the designer may have for brick, the key to its use in interior design is appropriateness.

5 Unit Masonry

Unit masonry is a construction element fabricated to a uniform size, usually following a modular system. Brick is a unit masonry, the first devised. Unit masonry is a large enough topic, however, to merit a chapter of its own. Equally venerable, adobe is a type of unfired brick of pre-Columbian origin familiar to use from indigenous buildings of the American Southwest. In certain locations, limestone has been obtained for centuries from below the water table. It often is so soft that it is easily sawn into modular blocks, which harden after some exposure to the air. Terra-cotta has been in use for millennia, but only comparatively recently has it been fabricated into lightweight hollow tiles for unit masonry. More recently, portland cement has been utilized to produce a whole family of concrete blocks. Gypsum is molded into blocks for interior fire-resistant walls; and glass block, the epitome of the thirties, is again fashionable after decades of neglect.

Concrete Block

With the possible exception of brick, concrete block is the most commonly used unit masonry. Concrete block is formed of a mixture of portland cement with fine and coarse aggregate and, as with any concrete, water for curing the cement. The main variations in concrete block lie with the aggregate. Because of the high cost of shipping and the inherent ease of small-scale manufacture, concrete block is generally a locally made product. Whatever is available in the region is used for aggregate: traprock (basalt), limestone, and, in industrial areas, cinders, the residue of burnt soft coal. While it is not incorrect to label concrete blocks made with cinder aggregate "cinder block," they are still classified as concrete block. In each case the color of the aggregate, along with the shade of the cement, is the major factor in determining the color of the block.

To make concrete block, a rather dry concrete mix is packed under hydraulic pressure into steel molds. Almost immediately the blocks are turned out onto pallets to be moved to sheds for curing. To produce a quality product, moisture must be introduced to prevent premature drying of the fresh block and to allow complete curing of the cement.

Sometimes these curing sheds are actually steam kilns. The combination of high temperature and high moisture speeds the curing process. After they are cured, blocks may be transported on the same flats to the building site by self-loading trucks.

If there is a typical concrete block, it is the one that has the nominal size of 8″ × 8″ × 16″ (200 × 200 × 400 mm). To maintain the building standard module while allowing for a ⅜″ (10 mm) mortar joint, the actual size will be 7⅝″ × 7⅝″ × 15⅝″ (194 × 194 × 397 mm). A variety of accessory blocks are produced: 8″ × 8″ × 8″ (200 × 200 × 200 mm) blocks, used primarily to start and end alternate courses in running bond; U blocks to form beams within the wall; jamb blocks to set windows or expansion joints; pilaster blocks to form columns within the wall; and many more proprietary products.

Concrete blocks are normally fabricated with voids (two or three) cast in their cores so that a section is only about 50 percent solid. These are still considered structural for ordinary load conditions. Solid blocks are available for unusually heavy loading conditions or for radiation protection. For various purposes, other thicknesses are made, maintaining the nominal 8″ × 16″ (200 × 400 mm) face: 4″, 6″, 12″ (100, 150, 300 mm). Only the 8″ and 12″ are considered structural. The same special shapes are generally available for these sizes.

TYPICAL CONCRETE BLOCK

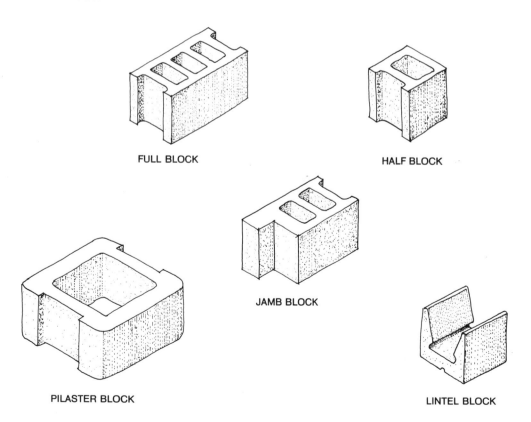

FULL BLOCK

HALF BLOCK

JAMB BLOCK

PILASTER BLOCK

LINTEL BLOCK

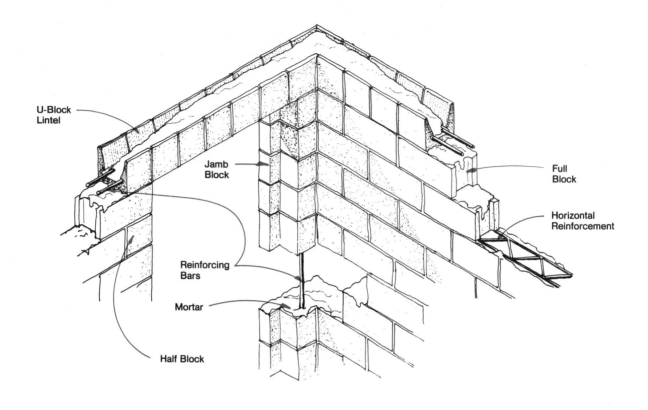

While a concrete block wall has considerable strength in direct bearing, it has little ability to resist side thrust. To counter this weakness, it is possible to strengthen concrete block walls far beyond their own inherent strength through the judicious use of steel reinforcement. Specially made joint reinforcement may be laid continuously along horizontal mortar joints, perhaps every second or third course. Ordinary concrete-reinforcement bars (rebars) may be set in vertically aligned block voids and filled with mortar or concrete. If greater strength is required, a fully reinforced concrete column can be formed using pilaster block. Lintels over openings and wall caps can be formed with U block, requiring no other formwork. With proper placement of rebars, a full-strength, integrally reinforced concrete beam can be created. In some areas precast reinforced concrete lintels are also available.

Ornamentation. As might be expected from a molded product, almost any degree of ornamentation may be developed for introduction into the block-manufacturing process. A standard block that is widely distributed has a 45-degree "V" recessed at one end that permits a great variety of patterns to be created on a wall including triangles, diamonds, and stripes. Paul Rudolph developed a double block with a row of holes separating the two parts. When this block is split through the line of holes, the face with the half holes has an interesting vertical ribbed texture. These blocks have remained on the market. A variety of pierced patterns have been developed to allow partial screening along with ventilation. In larger scale work, custom designs can be reasonably incorporated into the block. These can range from a simple frieze to a complete fantasy, exemplified by the Holyhock house in Los Angeles by Frank Lloyd Wright. The basis of economy in this custom work is the multiple reuse of the custom-made forms.

Special face finishes are available in great variety. Patent finishes rivaling ceramic glazes are factory produced. Most of them are based on portland cement with silicones, acrylics, and other plasticizers along with any desired pigments.

ORNAMENTAL BLOCK FACES

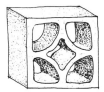 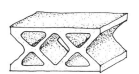 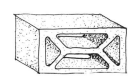 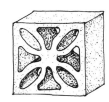

LATTICE BLOCKS

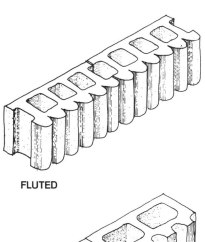

FLUTED

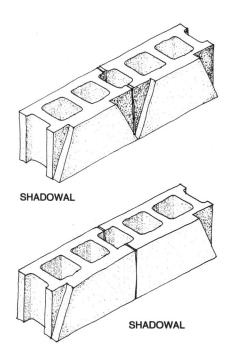

SHADOWAL

SHADOWAL

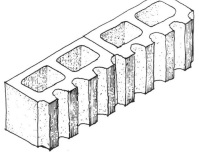

RIB OR SPLIT

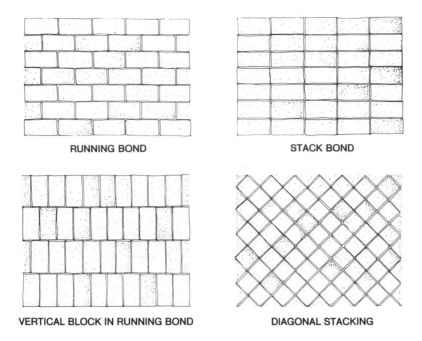

RUNNING BOND

STACK BOND

VERTICAL BLOCK IN RUNNING BOND

DIAGONAL STACKING

As with brick, the units can be laid in a variety of patterns. The units can be stacked horizontally, vertically, and diagonally. The limits lie only with the imagination of the designer. Since blocks are usually laid in a single wythe, all bonds are purely ornamental.

Lightweight and insulating block are both made of the same material; they are named for the function desired. Made with lightweight aggregate bound with the usual cement paste, they are both lighter and less heat-transmitting than ordinary stone aggregate block. The lightweight aggregates include expanded mica and expanded shale. The finished blocks are more than 40 percent air pockets, therefore they weigh about 40 percent less than stone blocks and increase their insulation value by 30 percent. While the higher insulation value has obvious benefits, the lighter weight is especially advantageous in high-rise building.

Mortar. Mortar for concrete blockwork is similar to that used for brick or stone, as is the mortar joint treatment. Organic adhesives for blockwork are available but rather seldom used; unless specially sized blocks are used, modularity is lost by the thinner joints. A new block-laying process consists of stacking the block without mortar and surface-coating them with plasticized fiberglass-reinforced-cement plaster to create a unified wall. This system relies upon the ability of the coating to take considerable tensile stress to stabilize the wall. When a block wall is plastered with ordinary mortar, the process is called parging; this is done to improve the water resistance of a wall below grade, or to provide a stucco finish.

Cleaning and Sealing. A concrete block wall is not inherently waterproof. If a natural finish is desired, the wall should be cleaned, lightly honed with a carborundum block, and coated with a suitable sealer. This latter treatment not only improves water resistance but reduces soiling, or at least facilitates cleaning. A common sealer is a 6 percent silicone solution. Other sealers are based on stearates or waxes. Sealers do not change the appearance of a wall except, perhaps, for a slight darkening. They also do not last indefinitely and must be periodically reapplied. Concrete block takes paint well, but because of the inherent porosity of the block, latex paint is the preferred choice over oil-based paint, which has a tendency to peel when water penetrates from behind. Cement base paint is an excellent choice, as it improves water resistance and is quite permanent.

Structural Clay Tile

Made of fired clay, of the same type as brick, structural clay tile was once extensively used, especially in commercial construction. Today, the less expensive concrete block has largely driven it from the market. Clay tile still has its uses, however, as a lightweight weather-resistant product capable of being finished with tough ceramic glaze.

Like some bricks, structural clay tiles are produced from prepared clay by the extruded stiff-mud and wire-cut processes. Consequently, they come with a variety of cross-sectional designs. Some are made with a striate surface meant to key plaster; others have a built-in grip to facilitate handling. All have a relatively small solid-to-void ratio. The walls of structural clay tile are called shells; the hollows, cells; and the inner dividers, webs. The most common face size is normally 12″ × 12″ (300 × 300 mm). Thicknesses range from 2″ through 12″ (50 to 300 mm).

This apparently delicate structure is sufficiently load-bearing for low-rise structures, especially when the tile is reinforced by plastered surfaces. Bonding the plaster with the tile is facilitated by the striate surfaces and the natural porosity of the material. This porosity is sometimes enhanced by mixing into the clay sawdust or coal particles, which burn away during firing.

Glazed structural clay tiles are heavier in weight, since they cannot rely upon plaster for reinforcement. They are proprietary products, and complete information is available only from the manufacturer. In general, they are modular in size with the nominal 4″ × 8″ (100 mm × 200 mm), 6″ × 12″ (150 mm × 300 mm), and 8″ × 16″ (200 mm × 400 mm) predominating. Thicknesses range from 2″ (50 mm) for facing only, glazed one side, through 4″, 6″, and 8″ (100 mm, 150 mm, 200 mm). These may be glazed on both sides for a finished wall.

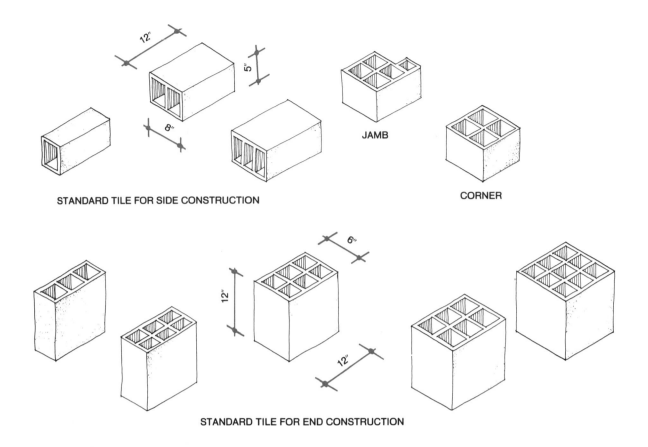

STANDARD TILE FOR SIDE CONSTRUCTION

JAMB

CORNER

STANDARD TILE FOR END CONSTRUCTION

A great many special shapes are produced to obtain a finished work: half blocks, coved bases, rounded jamb or corner blocks, glazed end blocks; entire catalogs full. The designer is usually sent shop drawings for approval with every required block identified. Glazes are available in all colors and textures. The finished wall is durable, cleanable, sanitary, and institutional in feeling.

Gypsum Block

Gypsum, known in chemistry as hydrous calcium sulfate, has inherent high fire resistance that can make it very desirable as partition block where fire protection and sound control are important. The material is not strong enough for load bearing. It is easily cut and patched, laid in gypsum mortar, and invariably plastered. Relatively light in weight, the blocks are large, 12″ × 30″ × 2″, 3″, 4″, and 6″ thick (300 × 760 × 50, 75, 100, and 150 mm). The thinner blocks are solid; the thicker blocks may have core voids, often circular in cross section. The thickness selected is dependent upon the height of the wall and the degree of fire or sound resistance desired. Gypsum blocks often have added a small percentage of wood chips as reinforcement or expanded shale to make them even lighter.

The block wall becomes a surface for plaster, which adheres directly to it very well. The plaster is essential to the stability of the wall. Although nails can be driven into this wall for some construction purposes, heavy loads can be attached only by bolting through the block.

Glass Block

Glass block can be viewed as unit masonry that transmits light. Molded in half sections, two pieces are heat-sealed together to form each block. In the process, a partial vacuum is created in the hollow. The edges are made concave and roughened to receive mortar. Again, glass block is a proprietary product and the manufacturer must be consulted. Common sizes are 5″ × 5″ and 8″ × 8″ (125 × 125 mm and 200 × 200 mm). Less common is a 12″ × 12″ (300 × 300 mm) size. All sizes are 3⅞″ (100 mm) thick.

A variety of surface finishes are available ranging from nearly clear through obscure to diffusing. Color is available as is insulating block, the latter containing a fine web of fiberglass to reduce convection with minimal reduction of light transmission.

Glass blocks are laid in normal mortar with joint reinforcement every two or three courses. Joints are usually tooled concave. For exterior walls, provision must be made around the perimeter for expansion and contraction, which is considerable if temperatures range widely. Glass block walls are never load-bearing.

Blocks of solid glass, optically clear, are available for higher security and protection against vandalism. They are very heavy and expensive.

GLASS BLOCK

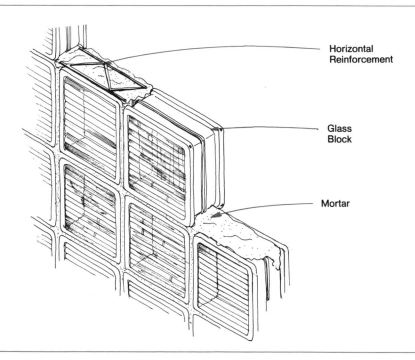

Horizontal Reinforcement

Glass Block

Mortar

Unit Masonry in Interiors

Few designers find the materials discussed in this section particularly attractive as interior finishes, with the exception of glass block. This judgment is not merely subjective; concrete block has been used in institutional and low-prestige spaces so extensively that the public associates the material with undesirable environments. While tactilely a rough and utilitarian material, when used honestly, concrete block has been used in creating some landmark designs of modern architecture. But even painted or glazed, it does not convey a sense of luxury. It is frequently used in dormitories, commercial buildings, and residential basements, usually for economy. Budget permitting, most designers would specify a material other than concrete block.

Adobe has an even rougher texture than concrete block. It still has a sentimental following in the Southwest, where there are a few serviceable traditional adobe buildings left. The uneven texture can be pleasing to designers and clients alike who will take great trouble to preserve the effect.

Structural clay tile represents only another plaster surface to designers and is rarely used in new construction. This material tends to evoke the same disaffection that concrete block generates.

Gypsum block has been used extensively in the past for interior partitions in commercial structures because of its fire resistance. But as a finish material it is again considered only another plaster surface. Unlike other masonry units, gypsum block is too soft to leave exposed. In recent times, most commercial buildings have used metal stud systems with gypsum wallboard for partitioning. Layered, the gypsum board can obtain any level of fire resistance desired.

Glass block has become the symbol of Art Deco. With the renewed interest in this style, along with the development of Postmodernism in the 1970s, glass block has become a favored material again. It provides a remarkably functional finish: it never needs painting, is easily cleaned, and is pleasant to the touch. However, compared to other interior partitions or finishes, glass block is costly. That alone gives it an aura of luxury; indeed, it can be seen frequently in some of the most elegant interiors that are being built today. Glass block has been singled out as a featured material by some of the leading Modern and Postmodern architects and designers.

It is important to be familiar with the dimensions of blocks and to understand the limits of their aesthetic appeal. If used intelligently and assembled sensitively with other materials, any of the types of unit masonry can become an attractive tool in the hands of a skilled designer.

6 Ferrous Metals

Ferrous metals are metals largely composed of the element iron, usually in the forms called iron or steel.

Iron as a basic element is a soft, chemically-active yellowish metal so rare in unalloyed form that it is found only as a laboratory curiosity. In practice it is loosely bound with carbon and slag (smelting residue). Iron is used as a construction material in two basic forms: cast and wrought. Steel is a more refined alloy of iron.

Properties of Iron and Steel

Cast iron is made directly from pig iron, as drawn from the smelting furnace, remelted and poured into molds. Dark to silver gray in color, cast iron is highly crystalline in structure, hard, and brittle.

Wrought iron is forged (hammered), which draws the crystals of iron, carbon, and slag into long fibers. It is fibrous in structure, and is lighter gray in color, more malleable, and tougher than cast iron.

Steel is defined as an alloy of iron and carbon, though it contains less carbon than "iron." The carbon, which comprises less than 2 percent of steel, is carefully controlled and more finely distributed than in iron; the slag is eliminated. Steel is silvery in color and tougher than iron, whether cast or wrought (rolled or forged). Today many metals are used to alloy iron; they are all collectively referred to as steel.

Iron is mentioned in Homer's *Odyssey*; it may be an anachronism, as iron was not in general use until later. Iron in quantity seems to have come into Western history for arming the Doric invasions of Greece about 1200 B.C. Indeed, iron seems to be the main reason for the success of that venture, not only because it made harder weapons than the bronze of the defenders. Once the technique of smelting ore was understood, iron became plentiful, because the ore was widely available.

For the next 2,500 years iron was still too scarce for use beyond weapons and other tools. The Industrial Revolution represents, more than anything else, the mass production of iron. Beginning with England in the eighteenth century, the Coalbrookdale Bridge represents the first use of iron as a structural material. The railroads increased demand for iron and the newly mass-produced steel.

Steel was developed in the Middle East with the ever-increasing quality of wrought iron through gradually improved forging techniques. These removed more and more of the carbon and all of the slag until the optimum alloy was attained. Damascus was believed to be the source of the ultimate sword blade, and "Damascene" steel came to European manufacture with the Moors to Spain, centering in Toledo. Steel remained a handcrafted product until Bessemer developed his converter in England in the nineteenth century. In the Bessemer converter, air blown through molten pig iron oxidizes most of the carbon. Most of the remaining impurities are formed into a slag that is drawn from the top. The carbon is expelled as the gas carbon dioxide; other impurities oxidize into the floating slag. Carbon can then be added in controlled quantities to bond intimately to the iron. Today, most steel is produced by the open-hearth process or the electric furnace. In more recent times metallurgists have developed steels with many properties by the addition of trace metals. There is now a great variety of steels to choose from for a given task.

For a few great decades in the mid-nineteenth century, the plentiful availability of cast iron sparked a renaissance for designers. Reusable patterns of wood packed into separable sand molds enabled the mass-production of columns, bases, capitals, and ornamentation. Even entire building façades were assembled with a hitherto unknown ease and thrift. Examples of this age abound, notably in the SoHo area of New York City. Cast iron columns replaced load-bearing masonry walls for the interior of structures, freeing great amounts of floor space. Before, economical building heights were limited to nine or ten stories because the space for additional floors was lost due to the necessary thickening of the masonry of the lower floors. With cast iron, the skyscraper became possible. The cast iron façade fell out of fashion before being replaced by the curtain wall. Today cast iron is little used in construction except for a few odd fittings and some trelliswork that is not yet plastic.

Wrought iron gained flexibility and tensile strength by the process of forging. For a long time it served as a rude steel. Since the late nineteenth century, however, the availability of modern steel has replaced it for most purposes except where its higher resistance to corrosion is important. It is still used for piping and forged ornamental ironwork.

Rolled structural steel is equally strong in tension and compression; it is ten times stronger than the highest quality wood. Available in unlimited sizes, steel was born for building construction. The first steel structural sections were riveted together from sheared or torch-cut rolled plate. The requirements of the spreading railroads, which had started with wood rails on stone ties in the early nineteenth century, brought about the first rolled steel section, the railroad track rail. Recognized as a fairly good structural section, these rails were soon incorporated into building construction, particularly into floor structure.

CAST IRON FAÇADES, COLUMNS, BASES, AND CAPS

RAIL WITH BRICK ARCH FLOOR

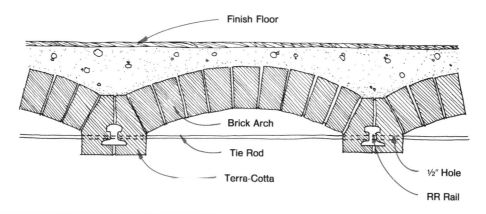

The building industry began to rival the railroads in demand for steel, and the industry soon catered to this demand by producing ever more various and efficient structural shapes. The first series of sections produced especially for building construction became known as the American Standard Beam, or I beam. A series of shapes known as channels, angles, tees, and zees were initiated for boxcar construction, but soon found their uses in building. The unbalanced axes of the I beam prompted the development in the early twentieth century of the wide-flange section (symbol "W") for columns. Soon the ever-greater spans demanded of beams proved the lateral weakness of the I beam, and the wide-flange section became the most prevalent beam.

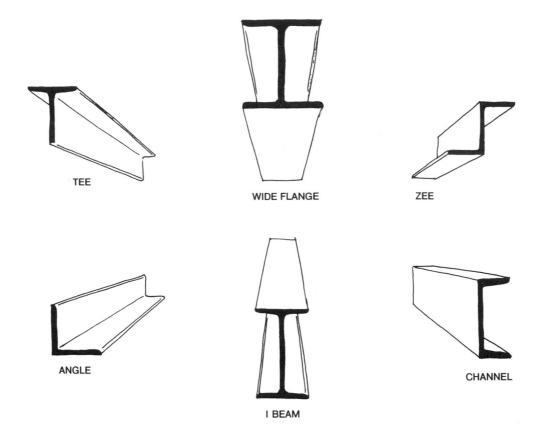

TEE

WIDE FLANGE

ZEE

ANGLE

I BEAM

CHANNEL

Steel in Construction

With the great variety of structural sections available, the steel frame structure was developed in Chicago near the turn of the century. The first steel frame structure (although the columns were still cast iron) is conceded to be the twelve-story 1885 Chicago office of the Home Insurance Company of New York by the architect William LeBaron Jenny.

Round columns, now steel, are still popular in one- or two-story structures. They are the most efficient column form: symmetrical about all axes. The difficulty of making connections to the curved surface, however, makes the wide-flange shape preferred for higher rise buildings. The usual technique for skeletal frame construction is to run the columns continuously from foundation to roof and hang the beams and girders from them. As you ascend the structure, the loads on the columns diminish, so lighter sections are used on succeeding floors.

Rolled sections are produced in depths ranging from 6″ (150 mm) to as deep as 30″ (760 mm). Each depth is available in a variety of weights, which are essentially determined by the number of passes the steel makes through the forming rollers. The width of the flange is also variable. Beyond these off-the-shelf shapes, it is possible to have any size beam fabricated from rolled sheets.

Steel is a homogeneous structural material; that is, its strength in tension is equal to its strength in compression. The special quality of steel is its tensile strength, by which figure the particular steel is identified. Common structural steel is low carbon, or "mild" steel, and presently has a working strength of 22,000 psi or pounds per square inch (1,550 kg/cm). Twenty years ago this value was only 20,000 psi (1,400 kg/cm), and earlier it was lower still. This does not mean that mild steel is increasing in strength as the years go by; the ultimate strength has remained at about 75,000 psi (5,250 kg/cm). The allowable working strength is about one-third the ultimate strength to allow for flaws in the manufactured product. The increasing strength is allowed because of continuously improved quality controls resulting in a more dependable product. When working with an older building, you should be sure to know the allowable strength at the time it was built. Only then can structural changes be calculated.

Steels of higher working strength are available when required for particular reasons. However, they must be used with discretion because the cost of these high-strength steels is disproportionately higher than the increased strength. There are occasions where weight savings, increased headroom, or unusual span or load conditions may justify the increased cost.

Very deep plate girders are in a class of their own. Principally used in bridge construction, they are occasionally used in building where very heavy load conditions or very long spans are involved.

Steel rods have long been used as the tension members of trusses when wood was used for the compression members. Completely steel trusses were one of the earlier uses of smaller rolled steel shapes, principally the double-angle truss with gusset plate construction.

INCREASING WEIGHTS PER UNIT OF LENGTH IN ROLLED SHAPES

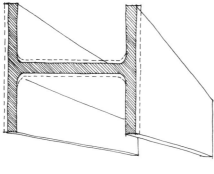

INCREASING WEIGHT
IN W SHAPE

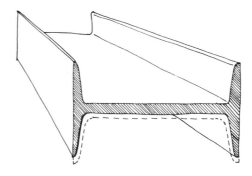

INCREASING WEIGHT
IN S SHAPE

STEEL BAR JOISTS

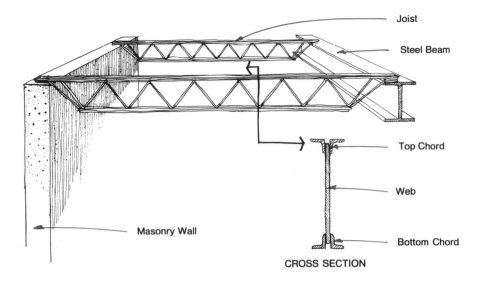

STEEL ALLOYING ELEMENTS

ELEMENT	AMOUNT	EFFECT
Carbon	Less than .9% More than .9%	Increases strength and hardness Increases hardness and brittleness
Manganese	.5 to 2%	Increases strength and hardness
Silicon	Less than 2.5%	Increases strength and hardness
Sulfur	Less than .05% .05 to 3%	Malleable at high temperatures Improved machinability
Phosphorus	Less than .05%	Increases strength and rust-resistance
Copper	Less than .25%	Increases strength and rust-resistance
Chromium	4 to 12% More than 12%	Increases strength at high temperature Increases corrosion-resistance
Nickel	1 to 4% Up to 27%	Increases strength and toughness Stainless steel
Molybdenum	.1 to .4% Up to 4%	Increases toughness and hardness In stainless, increases corrosion-resistance
Tungsten	17 to 20%	Increases strength
Vanadium	.15 to .2%	Promotes small grain size

While this type of truss is custom built, a very popular standardized steel structural element is the bar joist. Essentially a relatively shallow truss that is usually flat, the bar joist is available in depths from 16" (400 mm) to 36" (900 mm) or more. Normally spaced 24" (600 mm) on center, bar joists can span 40' (12 m) or more.

Cable structures are best able to exploit the high tensile strength of steel. The most familiar, and oldest, such use is the suspension bridge. From high piers, great cables hang in catenary curves, anchored to the shores. Lighter cables, in turn, hang from the great cables to suspend the roadbed; the latter is stabilized by plate girders. Suspension systems have been used in recent years for roofs with very long spans, such as stadiums. Even more recently, steel cables have been used to anchor and stabilize air-support structures.

The problem of corrosion (rust) is so severe with steel that methods of controlling it through alloying have been sought. Copper-bearing steel, that is, steel alloyed with about .25 percent copper, has been found to have increased corrosion resistance. Steel alloyed with a much higher percentage of chromium will also resist corrosion. Stainless steel is almost completely corrosion-resistant, but requires a great deal of expensive alloy metals. The most popular blend is "18–8," which is 18 percent chromium and 8 percent nickel. Too costly to be used structurally (except in the Barcelona pavilion), stainless steel is mostly used for hardware, kitchen fixtures, and interior furnishings.

Weathering steel is an alloy that, when exposed to the weather, quickly forms an iron oxide coating that is indistinguishable from any other rust. Within two or three years, however, this coating will develop into a grayish film that resists further corrosion. Care must be taken to prevent staining of the surround during the earlier stage, and to weather artificially, if necessary, protected areas. This attractive and recently popular solution to corrosion is of questionable value in high-salt-air or industrial-pollution regions.

Sheet ferrous metals, outside of the mechanical-equipment field, are principally used as sheathing, flooring, and roofing. For corrosion protection, these sheet metals are often galvanized, coated with baked or porcelain enamel, or both. Applied under factory conditions, these finishes may be considered durable.

Ferrous metal sheets are often deformed to make them more structurally rigid. These deformations may take the shape of corrugations, standard forms, and many proprietary shapes. They may be made up as "sandwich" panels with insulation and interior surfacing.

Lightweight steel framing is a system much in use for non-load-bearing partitions. Rolled from galvanized sheet steel into a channel shape, the partitions are made in the same dimensions as light wood framing lumber. The partitions are also built up in much the same manner as wood frame: 16" (400 mm) on center studs are set into sole plates and capped with a top plate. They are assembled with self-

SHEET METAL FORMS

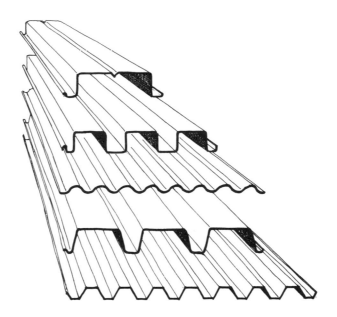

LIGHT METAL FRAMING

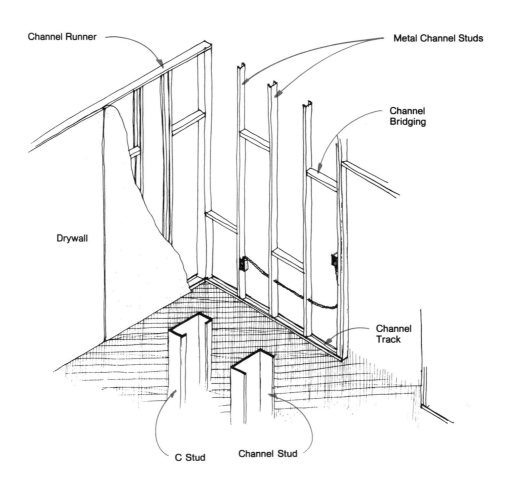

Channel Runner

Metal Channel Studs

Channel Bridging

Drywall

Channel Track

C Stud

Channel Stud

drilling, self-tapping screws. Finish materials are fastened with similar screws. Light steel framing members are perforated to permit easy installation of electrical conduit and minor plumbing.

Connections. From the beginning of iron and steel structures, riveting has been the most common method for assembly of the parts. In shop work the holes are punched by a hydraulic press, the plates are aligned, and red hot rivets with one head are inserted. A second rivet head is then formed by hydraulic pressure and the plates are squeezed tightly together. In the field, the holes have usually been shop-punched and the plates temporarily aligned with a drift pin. The heated rivet is tossed to the crew, who insert it and form the second head with a pneumatic hammer. This daring work, often on a high, skeletal perch, has all but passed into history. Shop-riveting is still used occasionally.

Aside from the dangers inherent in field riveting, the disadvantages of riveting are the need for overlapping plates, which requires extra material, and the hole punching. The hole punched through a steel plate for riveting effectively removes a strip of metal that is, structurally, the width of the hole. The greatest advantage of rivets is their dependability. A tap with a hammer will tell the experienced inspector whether the rivet is sound or not. If the designer is unhappy with any exposed rivet heads, they can be treated in various ways.

RIVETED JOINTS AND HEAD TREATMENT

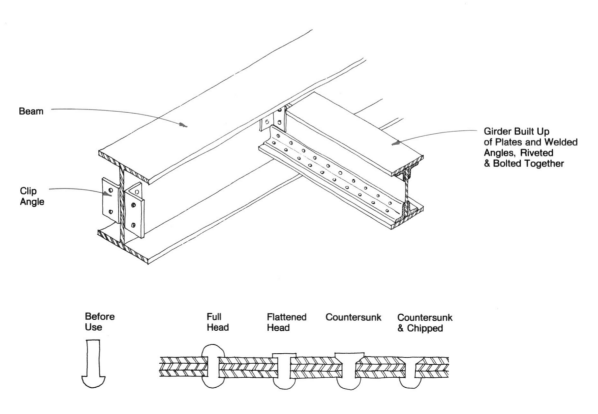

Beam

Clip Angle

Girder Built Up of Plates and Welded Angles, Riveted & Bolted Together

Before Use   Full Head   Flattened Head   Countersunk   Countersunk & Chipped

Since the 1960s, welding has supplanted riveting to a large extent for ferrous metals. Steel may be welded by an oxyacetylene process when the job is small or when portability of equipment becomes important. However, most welding is done by the electric arc process: A flux-covered rod is held near the surface and a high-energy electric arc is generated. The resultant heat melts together the end of the rod and the edges of the joint material. Effectively, the welding causes the separate pieces to become one.

Welding has many advantages over riveting: no overlapping, no loss of structural material, a neat appearance. The appearance can be further enhanced by grinding and polishing, as the works of Mies van der Rohe demonstrate. Shop-welding is often done in a semiautomated fashion with a track for the welding machine to run along at the correct speed. The most popular type of weld for when pieces are at right angles is the fillet. When two plate are joined, the edges are usually vee-cut and butt-welded. When a plate is hung against a structural member, holes may be prepared in the plate and the plate plug-welded to the structural member.

The great disadvantage with welding is the difficulty in inspecting the work for soundness. A poor weld can look fine; certainly a hammer blow will tell you nothing. If the weld is structurally critical, X-ray equipment can be brought to the job at great expense. This also necessitates clearing all workers from the project, because the energy required for an X ray to penetrate heavy steel can only be dealt with by remote control. For most jobs quality control is dependent upon the strict use of certified welders, with some reliance upon the safety factors always used in structural design.

TYPICAL WELDS

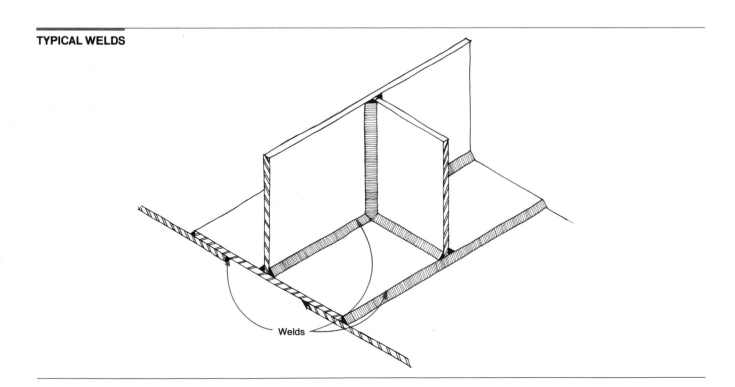

Welds

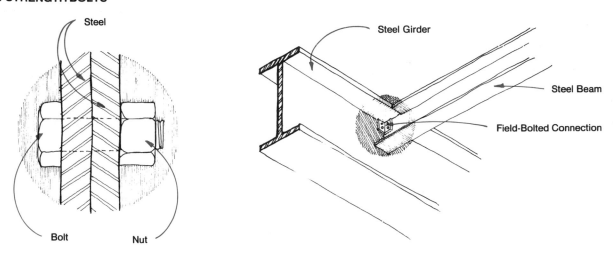

The use of high-strength bolts has eliminated the rivet almost entirely from field steel erection. Connection devices are shop-riveted or welded; holes are prepunched. During erection, parts are aligned temporarily with drift pins, and the high-strength bolts are inserted. The nuts are tightened to a specified degree by a torsion wrench to avoid overstressing the bolts. The great advantage to this system is its simplicity. A pocket full of bolts and nuts and a torsion wrench are all that is required for the steel erection.

Fire and Steel. A distinction must be made between fire-resistant construction and noncombustible construction. A steel structure is certainly the latter, but not the former. Steel is noncombustible because it contributes no fuel to the fire, but is not fire-resistant because heat reduces its structural strength. At about 800 to 900 degrees Fahrenheit (430 to 480 degrees Celsius) steel begins to weaken. By 1,200 degrees Fahrenheit (650 degrees Celsius) the steel structure will collapse under its own weight. Even a small fire can attain these temperatures. The operative building code is the sole determining source for the required fire protection, based upon use and occupancy, and that protection is expressed as one- to four-hour fire resistance; the term "fireproof" is no longer used. This fire resistance is actually tested in the Underwriter's Laboratory by installing a sample building system against an opening in a standardized furnace. The resistance is determined by the length of time it takes the fire to burn through the system.

To attain a required fire resistance steel must be protected. Early structural steel was enclosed with brick or structural clay tile, often specially molded to conform to the structural shapes. Today concrete, frequently lightweight, is popular, as is gypsum block. Gypsum board is an economical solution and can be easily layered to any level of fire resistance required. Sprayed-on finishes are a convenient solution, now that safer materials have been substituted for asbestos. Great care must be exercised with the spray systems to prevent damage or removal by other trades in the course of their work, which can be so easily concealed. There are also suspended ceiling systems available that will give a certain fire rating to a steel structure above.

Corrosion. Rust is a self-generating chemical reaction; once started it will spread out in all directions, rust breeding rust. Dampness, high humidity, salt spray, and atmospheric pollution will speed the process.

Iron, whether cast or wrought, is fairly resistant to this corrosion. The discontinuity caused by the crystals or strands of carbon and slag reduces the spread of any rust that has started. Rust will occur, but it may take centuries to reach the point of destruction. Steel, with the exception of the special alloys mentioned above, is especially prone to rust and must be protected. Structural steel, as stored in the yard, must be expected to have a film of rust from the start. Paint is the most common protection. After fabrication, the steel is given a coat of "long oil" primer (based upon tung or fish oil), which arrests the further growth of rust—at least for a time. For steel that is to be covered by other construction, a touch-up of the primer is considered adequate. If the steel is to be exposed, one or two coats of paint, preferably long-oil based, should be applied over the touched-up primer. This may hold up for years under optimum (dry, salt- and pollution-free) conditions. Inevitably the painting will have to be redone, frequently under less-than-optimum conditions.

For longer lasting protection, the erected steel can be sandblasted to remove all trace of rust, then immediately primed with finish coats. There are also longer lasting paints, such as the epoxies, that can be considered.

Galvanizing is an extremely effective corrosion protection. The steel is first pickled in an acid bath to remove all traces of rust, then dipped in molten zinc to coat all surfaces. This rust protection is maintained even when scratches and minor damage occur by means of an electrolytic reaction between the zinc and the exposed steel. With the proper primer, galvanized surfaces can also be painted for cosmetic purposes. The size limitations of the vats make the galvanizing of very large steel pieces impractical.

Ferrous Metals in Interiors

Steel is the principal ferrous metal used in interiors, but, with the exception of stainless steel, it is used more in furniture and partition systems than as a surfacing material. Stainless steel is used extensively in kitchens and laboratories for its resistance to corrosion, its durability, and its ease of maintenance. For these reasons it is also used for surfacing and hardware. Stainless steel is a great favorite for elevator doors, and, in often fanciful forms and textures, for elevator cab interiors. An expensive material that does not connote warmth, stainless steel is used at times in highly sophisticated office interiors. It may appear as wall surfacing or even laminated to doors and cabinets.

Steel is used frequently in fabricating furniture. From some use in the late eighteenth century, increasing through the nineteenth century, steel became the material of choice of the masters of modern design in the 1920s when they put their hands to furniture. Some steel designs of Marcel Breuer, Mies van der Rohe, and Le Corbusier are still in production. During the same period wrought iron furniture also became fashionable. Cheaper to fabricate than steel, wrought iron was used for less expensive furniture. It is still used extensively for outdoor furnishings, which are often a mere echo of the beautifully crafted objects of earlier times. Cast iron is the least-used ferrous metal in interiors today. While now rarely used for furniture, it was quite popular earlier in the century for bases of chairs, especially for school and auditorium seating.

BERTOIA CHAIR

Steel is, of course, in much use in offices in the form of furniture and file cabinets, which have a paint finish baked on by factory process. Hundreds of thousands of gray or green file cabinets and office desks from the early years are still surviving, especially in governmental agencies, attesting to the durability of steel furniture. Beyond this predictable use, some extremely handsome steel furniture has been made. Herman Miller and Knoll have pioneered the development of high-quality, well-designed office furniture. Steelcase, the largest office furniture manufacturer in the world, is the producer of the early Frank

Lloyd Wright designs. Knoll still carries some of the classic furniture designed at the Bauhaus in the twenties. There is also a great deal of furniture designed for the residential market using steel or wrought iron. Coffee tables, cabinet bases, and seating units are among the examples of ferrous metals used in the home.

Long before the advent of systems furnishings, office partitions were made of steel, or steel in combination with glass and other materials. They were often referred to as "bank partitions," and, indeed, many banks did use steel-and-glass partitions to give privacy to their employees. All of these assemblies were factory-made and demountable, with the same advantages that present-day systems furnishings have: They are easily moved and changed, and reusable for many years. Steel is still the material of choice for most systems-furnishings frames, but unlike their predecessors, they are designed for acoustical control. Screens and partitions for systems furnishings are now rarely surfaced with steel. Components such as shelving and drawers may be steel, but the vertical surfaces are usually fabric or some other sound-absorbing material.

Store and exhibition structures are major users of steel products. A number of handsome steel display systems exist that are particularly appropriate for exhibitions. Many store fixtures depend upon steel for their structure. Not to be forgotten are the many interior accessories traditionally of steel: lighting fixtures, ashtrays, desktop fixtures, and hardware.

7 Nonferrous Metals

Nonferrous metals are those containing little or no iron. Outside of gold and nickel-iron from meteorites, copper is the only metal found in its native state, that is, unoxidized and unsulfided. The earliest native copper was probably found in the arid regions of the Middle East, sometime in prehistory. The deliberate smelting of copper from ore was most likely discovered by accident under an ancient campfire. By 4000 B.C. copper was in common use for tools and weapons.

While copper is splendidly ductile, it is so soft that stone tools were in some ways still superior. Perhaps some copper was found naturally alloyed with other metals that made it harder. More likely the belief that gold was an alloy of copper set alchemists to work experimenting with various alloys. The discovery of bronze still belongs to prehistory, but it was in general use in the Mediterranean area by 2000 B.C. This alloy, about 85 percent copper and 15 percent tin, was no accidental discovery; copper and tin ores are seldom found in close proximity. The fascination of metallurgy is made understandable when it is seen that combining soft copper with even softer tin produces hard bronze.

The quest for gold no doubt led to the discovery of brass, an alloy of copper and zinc. While not as hard as bronze, brass is more workable and corrosion-resistant. Modern bronzes and brasses are made from copper with many alloying metals. The term bronze is applied to the harder products, brass to the softer.

The search for silver discovered the large number of white metals generalized as "pot" metals. Various combinations of lead, tin, and zinc, they are characteristically low in melting point, good in casting qualities, and corrosion-resistant. One of them, a mixture of lead and tin, was found to adhere well to other metals; so solder was born.

The most common nonferrous metal in building today is the most recent to become available. Although composing a large percentage of Earth's crust, aluminum is never found in the native state. It is also very difficult to extract from ores by conventional smelting techniques. It remained a laboratory curiosity until the process of electrolytic reduction was developed, along with plentiful sources of electricity. The urgency of aluminum production for aircraft in World War II brought the modern aluminum industry into being.

Aluminum

Second only to steel as the most used metal in the building industry, aluminum has only come into prominence in the last forty years. It is relatively strong, light in weight, and resistant to corrosion. In the pure state, aluminum is rather weak, but alloying it with a small percentage of manganese, silicone, or several other metals and combinations increases its strength considerably. Beyond that, tempering in the form of heat treatment further increases its strength.

While aluminum can be rolled into basic shapes by a process similar to that used for steel, because of its ductility it is more often extruded. The aluminum is forced through hardened steel dies to take any shape desired, solid or hollow. At least in two dimensions, this gives almost unlimited possibilities.

Aluminum is not used much for conventional frame structures. There are many factors involved. Aluminum weighs only about one-third as much as steel, which is a positive factor, but averages only about half steel's strength. Worse yet, the modulus of elasticity, the index of stiffness, is only about one-third that of steel. Aluminum is also difficult to weld, requiring special conditions and equipment. All of these problems could be dealt with but for the added factor of cost. Per pound, aluminum costs about four to six times as much as steel. Conventional structural use of aluminum is not ordinarily practical.

Where aluminum does find use is in less conventional structures. Buckminster Fuller embraced aluminum early on; aluminum tubing forms the basis for most geodesic structures, discontinuous compression structures, and space frames. Aluminum is most often assembled in these systems as compression members forced into cast fittings, with cables for required tension elements.

ALUMINUM EXTRUSIONS

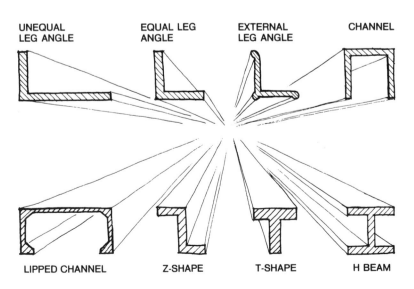

UNEQUAL LEG ANGLE   EQUAL LEG ANGLE   EXTERNAL LEG ANGLE   CHANNEL

LIPPED CHANNEL   Z-SHAPE   T-SHAPE   H BEAM

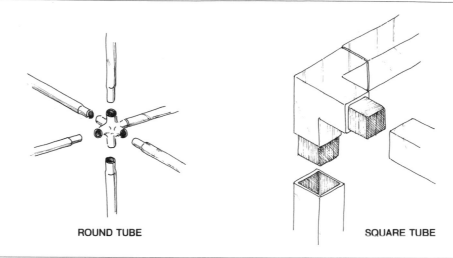

ROUND TUBE   SQUARE TUBE

The largest use for aluminum in building is in such nonstructural elements as windows, curtain walls, flashing, sheathing, and roofing. Its assets for these purposes include light weight, ease of forming complex sections, and resistance to corrosion. Aluminum is a good conductor, and while it is cheaper than copper, it surprisingly is not often used as electrical wiring. It seems that its susceptibility to electrolytic action and low melting point has made it suspect for this use.

Aluminum used in windows includes both operative sash and framing for fixed glass and show windows. Parts are usually assembled with self-tapping screws in prepared channels. Trimming parts to fit on the job is easily done with hand tools; tubular sections can be assembled around columns. Vinyl weatherstripping is built in to minimize leakage. Aluminum also has an excellent dimensional stability.

In severely cold climates the high level of conduction of heat through aluminum is its greatest disadvantage. This problem can be solved by including transmission breaks in the frames, with the parts joined by a low-conductance plastic.

The curtain wall, in its modern definition, may be said to have begun with Skidmore, Owings & Merrill's Lever House in New York City. Sheathing of high-rise buildings was mostly stone or brick before this landmark was built in 1952. The notion of including windows, spandrels, and all accessories into one aluminum assembly was a success often imitated, but never surpassed. Problems to be overcome included the fact that aluminum expands and contracts with temperature change. Consequently, over the entire face of a large building a great many working, yet waterproof, joints had to be made. Another problem was differential expansion between the various materials; aluminum, glass, and plastic had to be considered. By means of careful study, full-scale mock-ups, and extensive tests, all the problems were solved in advance. The first curtain wall was a successful one. For better or worse, the face of modern architecture has never been the same.

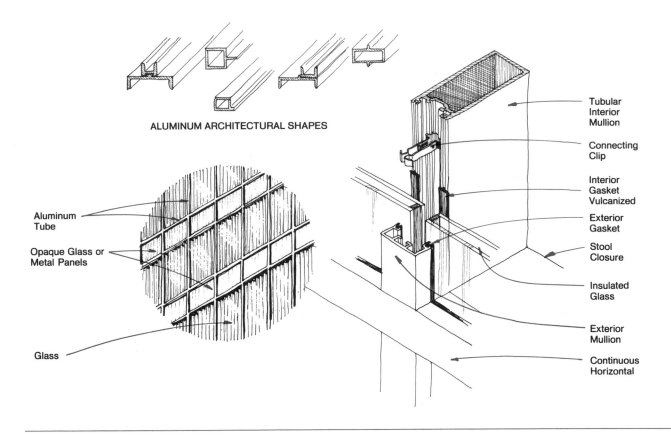

ALUMINUM ARCHITECTURAL SHAPES

Tubular
Interior
Mullion

Connecting
Clip

Interior
Gasket
Vulcanized

Exterior
Gasket

Stool
Closure

Insulated
Glass

Exterior
Mullion

Continuous
Horizontal

Aluminum
Tube

Opaque Glass or
Metal Panels

Glass

Flashing is a good use of the qualities of aluminum. It is also an exemplary illustration of aluminum's faults. Aluminum's high resistance to corrosion and ease of bending are ideal for flashing, but the material's rather high index of expansion and electrolytic activity require special care.

Aluminum sheathing for roofs and walls would seem ideal considering the material's light weight and resistance to corrosion. It is not without problems, however. Its ductility and lack of compatibility with other metals require special consideration. A greater degree of deformation of the sheets is required, even to the extent of often pressing surface texture into the sheet to increase rigidity. Gasketing is necessary to separate incompatible metals. The most successful use of aluminum as sheathing has been the sandwich panel, which has sheet-aluminum surfaces bonded to a rigid core, often of insulating material.

The electrolytic reaction of certain metals when in contact will spontaneously generate an electric current between them. Heightened by the presence of salts and moisture, this reaction will corrode the contact surface. Aluminum is particularly susceptible to electrolytic reaction when in contact with zinc and cuprous metals. There is little activity with any of the ferrous metals, and none with stainless steel. Therefore, with aluminum, no zinc fittings should be used, including galvanized steel, nor any bronze or other cuprous metals. Aluminum fittings are fine, of course, but stainless steel is usually preferred for hardness and strength. If incompatible materials must be juxtaposed, an insulating material, such as bituminous felt, must be placed in between.

Aluminum is corrosion-resistant because a single layer of non-self-generating oxide naturally forms on the surface; this effectively prevents further oxidation. When delivered untreated from the rolling or extrusion process, the aluminum is called "mill finish." It will oxidize rapidly, but in a spotty and uneven manner.

To provide an even finish, an electrolytic process called anodizing was developed. Under controlled conditions, the mill finish is cleaned and subjected to an electric current in a chemical bath. The brightness disappears, but the even dull finish is permanent. Soon after the process was developed, it was discovered that color could be introduced into the process. Many colors are available, but dark gray and various tones of bronze are the most popular. If a bright metallic finish is desired, aluminum can be successfully chrome plated.

In painting aluminum, care must be taken to clean the surface thoroughly. Mill finish is always oily from the process. As with most metals, epoxy enamels seem to provide the most durable finish.

Copper and Copper Alloys

Copper has been used for roofing and flashing from ancient times. It solders well and has a fairly low index of expansion, although not so low that provisions are not needed to permit movement. After taking its initial verdigris coating (or statuary brown, according to the local air pollutants), copper settles down to a high resistance to further corrosion. Always a high-cost item, copper is usually restricted to projects with a generous budget. The largest use of copper in most modern buildings is in the electrical wiring and plumbing.

Brass is used principally for hardware and ornamentation. It requires a good deal of maintenance since it is prone to blackish tarnish. Polishing brass is a luxury most building owners are willing to forgo. Brass takes chrome plating well, and in that form is most commonly seen today. Some brass is used for larger sizes and longer runs of water piping, and plumbing fittings.

With the exception of the Seagram Building, the use of bronze is restricted in most buildings today to the dedication plaque. But Mies van der Rohe (or perhaps Philip Johnson) surprised the world by selecting bronze to sheath his late masterwork, using perhaps twice the normal annual quantity of bronze produced by this country for that one building. It did not set a trend, however, and followers have settled for bronze-anodized aluminum. Bronze is an excellent metal for hardware, and is available with many finishes, including oil-rubbed. This low-maintenance finish turns the metal statuary brown, limiting further corrosion. All cuprous metals may be polished and lacquered to prevent tarnish. If a softer sheen is desired, the surfaces can be wire-brushed to a satin finish. Bronze is often permitted to take its natural patina, a process frequently speeded or controlled by chemical means, such as the oil finish previously noted. All cuprous metals take plating by other metals well, and are the base for most chrome, nickel, silver, or even gold finishes; they are themselves plated on steel or pot-metal bases.

Pot Metals

So named for their low melting temperatures and ability to mix easily together to create many alloys of varying characteristics, pot metals are also sometimes referred to as "base" metals, as opposed to the "noble" metals: silver, gold, and platinum. Pot metals commonly used in construction include zinc, tin, and lead.

Zinc was once used as roofing metal; its use today is largely restricted to the galvanizing process and as an alloy. In the past, tin was used to plate black iron for what is still called a tin roof. With the addition of lead, such a coating is referred to as terneplate, which solders very well. Such roofing is seldom done today, however, and tin is no longer a factor in building except for solder and alloying.

Lead was once a common roofing metal, useful because of an extreme ductility that permitted it to be hammered to fit any odd shape. Its use is now largely restricted to solder and a few ornamental castings.

Nonferrous Metals in Interiors

By far the most widely used nonferrous metal in interiors is aluminum. Such commonly used elements as horizontal and vertical window blinds are mostly aluminum. Integrated ceiling systems, designed to accomodate lighting, mechanical services, and acoustical control in the same structure, are often principally of aluminum. Although available as a laminate for plywood or particle-board panels, aluminum is not widely used for wall surfacing.

Aluminum is used in various forms for furniture, as sheet material (laminated), castings, extrusions, and even, occasionally, spun. A famous example is the line of tables and chairs with cast aluminum pedestals designed by Eero Saarinen for Knoll. An equally famous line was designed in cast aluminum by Charles Eames for Herman Miller.

The anodizing process permits the use of color on aluminum, but anodized aluminum is not the preferred finish for the leading designers; more often it is polished. It is difficult to tell polished aluminum from stainless steel, except for the weight.

While not as strong as steel, aluminum is strong enough to be used as the structural component for interior partitions, as well as systems furniture. Used extensively for accessories, aluminum is found as desk-top elements and ashtrays, hardware and picture frames.

EAMES CHAIR

BARCELONA CHAIR

Of the cuprous metals, copper and bronze are less frequently used than brass. There are some rare furniture pieces in bronze, however, and copper is used for range hoods and light fixtures.

Brass is widely used in interiors, most prevalently in furniture; there are tables, serving carts, and even chairs of brass. Many component parts, such as legs and bases for cabinets, are also of brass. While brass does tarnish, especially in high humidity, many people appreciate the warm glow of the metal and are willing to polish and maintain their brass. Lacquer coating can alleviate this problem.

Many early furniture pieces have brass hardware, and brass is still used for contemporary hardware of all kinds. Brass is exceedingly popular for accessories; the relative ease with which it can be worked and shaped makes it a natural material for crafts. Handworked items from less developed countries and the products of industrial mass production both create demand for brass.

In the early postwar years brass was probably the most popular material for light fixtures, especially for those from Finland and the other Scandinavian countries. In recent years these have been much less in evidence. As in every aspect of design, materials tend to be fashionable at varying times. Except for aluminum, the nonferrous metals recently have not been much in demand.

8 Concrete

Concrete is a mixture of portland cement, water, and fine and coarse aggregates. This plastic paste, when placed in forms or molds and cured, combines chemically to create a stonelike product. The Ancient Romans were well acquainted with concrete. The culmination of their construction skills was the casting in concrete of the magnificent dome of the Pantheon (126 A.D.). Spanning 142' (43 m), it is still in excellent condition. This span was not exceeded until the twentieth century. Roman concrete was based upon pozzolana, a natural volcanic dust which, when mixed with slaked lime, produced a slow-setting cement. The knowledge of concrete manufacture did not survive the Western Empire; it was lost in the Dark Ages.

Modern concrete was discovered by an Englishman, Joseph Asdin, in 1824. He found that a mixture of limestone and clay, when properly processed, made a cement product resembling limestone from the quarries of the English Isle of Portland. Asdin was awarded a patent for hydraulic cement, a cement that would cure under water, which he called portland cement. It is essentially the same product that is used today.

The potential for increasing the structural capability of the new material was soon recognized. While strong in compression, concrete is weak in tension. If iron or steel rods, strong in tension, could be incorporated into the structure in the proper location, they would reinforce the concrete. August Perret was producing steel-reinforced concrete structures by 1905. Pier Luigi Nervi, with his "ferro cemento" structures, brought engineered reinforced concrete to its highest expression in the 1930s.

Properties of Concrete

Although only one ingredient of concrete, portland cement is the key unifying element. To make portland cement, a mixture of calcium, silica, alumina, and iron is ground to a fine powder. This mixture is then fed continuously into a rotary kiln where it is heated to above 2,400 degrees Fahrenheit (1,316 degrees Celsius). At this temperature chemical activity takes place, essentially creating calcium compounds of the metals. After the resultant clinker is ground to a fine powder, a small amount of gypsum is added to control the setting time. A high level of control is necessary at every step in the process. This is normal portland cement; the body established to set standards for building products, the American Society for Testing and Materials, designates it as ASTM Type I.

ASTM Type IA is called air-entrained cement. Right from the clinkering process small amounts of material are incorporated into the cement, which causes billions of tiny air bubbles to form in a single cubic foot of concrete (.3048 m³). This makes a concrete that is considered to be more resistant to frost action.

ASTM Type II is modified to cure more slowly and consequently release the heat of hydration over a longer period of time. These qualities are useful during high-heat periods and where great masses of concrete are being used. ASTM Type IIA is similar to ASTM Type II, but with the air-entraining agent included.

ASTM Type III may be used when more rapid curing is desired. This type of cement is called "high early strength" cement. Manufactured in part from a somewhat different mix of ingredients, ASTM Type III's fast-curing property is mainly gained by grinding the clinkers to an extra-fine powder. This hastens the hydration, but does not increase the ultimate strength of the concrete.

There are a number of other ASTM standard types of cement available for particular construction circumstances. All of these special products are somewhat more costly than "normal" Type I.

Standard portland cement is medium-gray in color. When this is not satisfactory, white (or very nearly white) cement is available. This is produced by carefully selecting the ingredients for color, and reducing the iron and manganese content. Considering the fact that 80 percent of concrete is composed of aggregate, using dark aggregate will not produce white, or even light, concrete. To produce these, the aggregates would have to be light in color, such as limestone. If special colors are desired, mineral pigments can be added to this light concrete.

Gravel and sand are the common designations for coarse and fine aggregates. These are misnomers because the qualitative aim of sand and gravel is to be composed of particles of uniform size. For concrete aggregate the opposite is desired. The greatest variety of particle size produces the most desirable concrete aggregate. If the particles are screened, it is to see that a proper mixture of size is included. Ideally, when fine and coarse are mixed, there will be every size from the smallest particle up through 1″ to 1½″ (25 to 38 mm) screen. The aggregates are stored separately so that the fine aggregate does not sift down through the coarse.

Since aggregate makes up the bulk of the mass of concrete, care must be taken to use material of sufficient hardness and strength, clean and free of organic materials. Since cement is the most expensive ingredient, and must fill all voids between the aggregate particles, proper grading will generate the most economical concrete.

Lightweight aggregates have qualities to consider. Normal stone concrete is calculated at about 150 lbs per cubic foot (2,400 kg per cubic meter); lightweight concrete is half that or less. Lightweight concretes may be classified as structural, nonstructural, or reduced structural. The former are usually expanded shale, the latter expanded mica. These introduce a good deal of air space into the concrete. In addition to decreasing the weight of concrete, lightweight aggregate increases the insulation value, which is very low for ordinary stone concrete.

An essential ingredient in any concrete is water, which is required for hydration: the chemical bonding of water molecules to the cement ingredients. Ideally, only enough water should be added to permit the total hydration of the cement. If properly cured, this would result in the strongest concrete. It would also be a very dry mix, difficult to place and harder yet to properly fill the forms. A compromise must be made; additional water makes a more workable mix. The cost of this compromise, however, is lower strength concrete. In order for the chemical processes to be controlled, the water must be reasonably pure. Excess acidity or alkalinity, or the presence of salts or organic material, could have deleterious effect upon the finished concrete. A good rule of thumb is that the water used should be good enough to drink.

While concrete is always a mixture of portland cement, fine and coarse aggregate, and water, certain additives, called admixtures, are sometimes included for various purposes. These are proprietary products intended to control some property of the concrete. They also may adversely affect other properties, so care must be taken with their use. Their purposes fall under the following general categories: to improve workability, to reduce separation of aggregates, to entrain air, to accelerate setting, and to retard setting time.

Concrete is rated according to its allowable compressive strength. Most structural concrete is rated at 3,000 psi. For footings and other less critical uses, structural concrete rated at 2,500 psi is available. Higher strength concrete is possible for critical applications.

Unlike steel, which is a reliable factory-produced product, concrete is created in the field, where many variables can affect the reliability of the material. The ultimate strength of concrete is largely based upon two factors: the water/cement ratio and the curing process. There are many considerations of strength that may be applied to concrete: compressive, tensile, shear, bond, and more. This complicated situation is simplified by the fact that all these strength considerations are related to the compressive strength. Concrete that is high in compressive strength is strong in all ways. The related strengths are therefore indexed to the compressive strength, and only a compression test need be made to determine the quality of concrete.

Not long ago the degree of strength of concrete was thought to be determined by the ratio of cement to aggregate. Actually, it is a function of the water/cement ratio. Excess water evaporates to leave a porous and weak concrete. The old system was true to the extent that more aggregate requires more cement paste to thoroughly coat and fill the space between the particles. Trying to accomplish this by thinning the paste with more water will yield a poor product.

Concrete in Construction

When the optimum water/cement ratio has been attained, and the concrete is placed, care must be taken to prevent evaporation of the water before complete hydration has taken place. This is what is meant by the term "curing." There are a number of ways to accomplish curing; the choice is largely based upon site conditions. The simplest method is to delay the stripping of the forms for a minimum of two weeks. This is particularly effective for columns and deep structural members where little of the concrete surface is exposed. In the case of slabs and other highly exposed surfaces, or where the forms must be quickly reused, all exposed surfaces must be kept wet. If below water level, the structure may be flooded. In most cases, spraying is necessary, sometimes after covering the surface with cloth or straw. More often, today, the wetted surface is covered with plastic sheeting to retard drying. A recent curing technique is to paint the freshly exposed surfaces with a latex sealant to slow the process of evaporation.

Steel Reinforcement. Concrete is used without reinforcement in some applications, such as mass foundations, where the only forces involved are compressive. In any case where tensile forces are encountered, steel reinforcement greatly increases the structural capacity of the material. Since mild structural steel has an allowable working strength of 22,000 psi, steel will represent a relatively small percentage of the mass of reinforced concrete. Steel reinforcement bars (rebars) range in size from ¼″ in diameter in ⅛″ increments up to 2¼″ (6 mm to 57 mm in 3 mm increments). Rebars are designated by the number of ⅛″ (3 mm) increments of diameter; i.e., ¼″ = #2, ⅝″ = #5, and so forth. Rebars are "deformed," rolled with many projecting bumps, to improve the bond, or adhesion, to the concrete. For slab reinforcement, welded wire mesh of several gauges of wire of various spacing is manufactured.

Reinforcement serves a second function: to handle temperature changes. Aside from steel added for structural requirements, there is "temperature" steel, which is placed in the concrete to control expansion, contraction, and the consequent cracking due to temperature changes. The amount of temperature steel required is a constant percentage of the area of concrete.

Tensile reinforcement is laid in the forms following the calculated lines of tensile stress. Shop drawings are prepared from the structural plans, the bars are cut and bent as required, and they are delivered to the site ready for placement. To assure the exact placement of the steel,

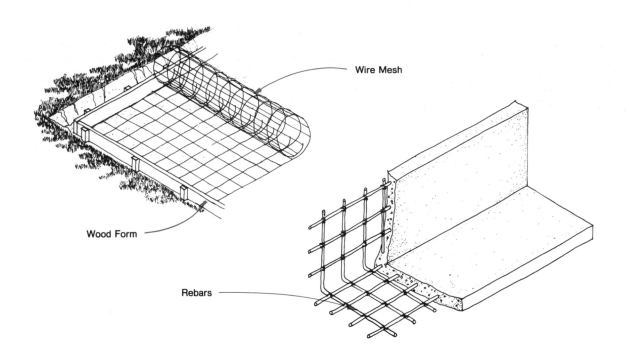

Wire Mesh

Wood Form

Rebars

TENSILE REINFORCEMENT BEAMS

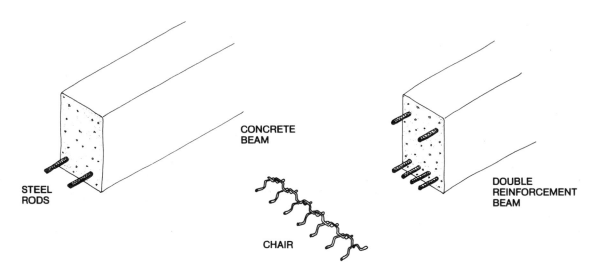

CONCRETE
BEAM

STEEL
RODS

CHAIR

DOUBLE
REINFORCEMENT
BEAM

"chairs" of fashioned wire are positioned in the forms and all pieces are wired together securely. The reinforcement must stay in place through all the vicissitudes to be endured on a construction site and the ungentle act of concrete placement.

Compressive reinforcement is used in beams and slabs when depth of section becomes critical. While concrete is good in compressive strength, square inch for square inch, steel is still six to ten times stronger in compression. Such beams are said to be double-reinforced.

Formwork. Concrete, like any plastic material, has no shape except that imposed upon it by forms. These are usually constructed of wood and must be built to support the weight of the fresh concrete, the hydraulic pressures of the still liquid material, and the burden of workers and equipment. In order to have a concrete structure, one must first build a wood structure, pour and cure the concrete, and then tear down the wood structure. Formwork constitutes a major item of expense in concrete construction; it is often the greatest expense. As a consequence, a great deal of ingenuity has been expended on saving cost for formwork. The key is in multiple use of the same forms. This may range from simple disassembly of job-built wood forms, and the reuse of the materials, to the fabrication of steel forms that may be reused many times. The economics of all this is not simple. The cost of forms must be traded off with the speed of construction, since the forms cannot be immediately stripped for reuse. For certain standardized structural systems, such as ribbed or waffle slabs, metal forms may be rented and returned.

Some of the more exotic solutions to the form problem include the use of heavy-gauge balloons to create domes and earth mounds to form concrete in many shapes, the balloons and earth to be removed later. Such a proposal was made as early as the fourteenth century for the dome of the cathedral of Florence; the earth was to be laced with coins to encourage removal by the citizenry. The dome was later built by Brunellesco using more conventional techniques. The earth-mound form was brought to a state of high art by Paolo Soleri in his desert houses.

FORMWORK

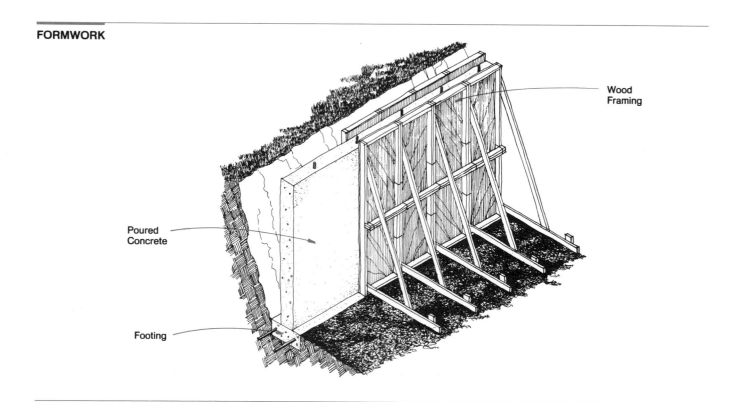

Wood Framing

Poured Concrete

Footing

Testing. Difficulties inherent in field conditions may call the reliability of any concrete work into question. There is no simple way to test concrete quality in the field; certainly visual inspection is not adequate. On larger projects, and where the strength of the concrete is critical, certain tests must be made.

The slump test determines the water/cement ratio. A standard cone-shaped mold is packed with concrete samples in a regulated manner; the concrete is then turned out on a flat surface. The amount the cone of concrete "slumps," or flattens, is measured. This determines the actual volume of water in the mix, which is affected by factors difficult to control, such as the moisture in the aggregate.

Compression-test cylinders may also be taken from time to time by packing samples of the concrete into a paper tube. The method is again very exactly prescribed. The cylinders are labeled with date and place, taken to the testing laboratory, cured for twenty-eight days, and then subjected to measured compressive force until crushed. Concrete is considered to have reached about 90 percent of its ultimate strength by then. If it is important to have quicker results, a seven-day test may be made; the concrete should then have reached about 60 percent of its ultimate strength.

SLUMP TEST

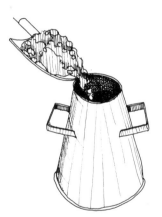

FILLING SLUMP CONE

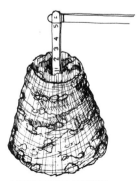

TAMPING CONE

LIFTING CONE

MEASURING SLUMP

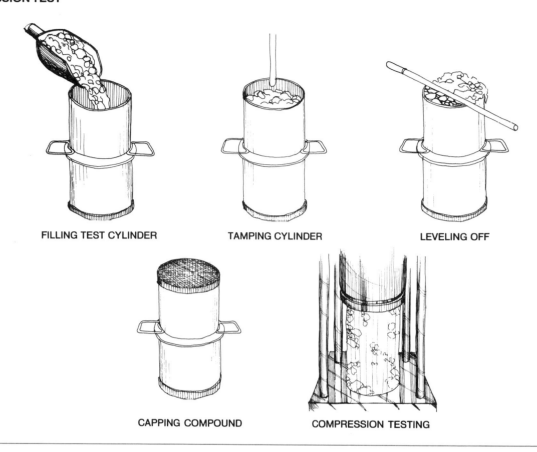

FILLING TEST CYLINDER   TAMPING CYLINDER   LEVELING OFF

CAPPING COMPOUND   COMPRESSION TESTING

What should be done if the concrete sample does not test to the strength upon which the structural design was based? First, cores can be cut from the actual structure and tested. If these are substandard, the structure may be loaded to exceed the design stress in hope that the safety factors inherent in all calculations will prevail. If all fails, there is nothing left but to demolish the work in the area of the faulty concrete and to try to determine the source of the error.

Joints. Concrete does not expand and contract with temperature changes as much as steel, but it does sufficiently to require that provisions be made. Concrete does not change with humidity like wood, but it does shrink as it loses excess water. This inevitably causes cracking, which may be controlled by control joints, or by scoring the surface deeply. Since cracking due to shrinkage cannot be avoided in concrete, steps must be taken to have the cracks take place in an orderly way. Control joints may penetrate the slab completely, limiting the shrinkage area, or they may create a weak (but straight) line in the slab for the shrinkage crack to follow. The number of joints required for complete control varies greatly under different conditions, but certainly the more there are the less likely it is that uncontrolled cracking will take place.

Great damage can occur to a large building if provision for expansion and contraction is not made. These expansion joints must extend

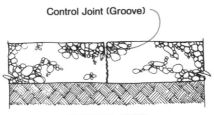

Control Joint (Groove)

CONTROL JOINT

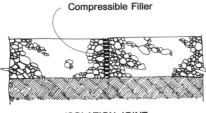

Compressible Filler

ISOLATION JOINT

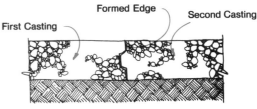

First Casting   Formed Edge   Second Casting

CONSTRUCTION JOINT

entirely through the building, essentially separating it into two or more adjacent structures. Many devices to cover these joints, which may be 1″ (25 mm) wide or more, have been developed. They all pose problems with which the designer must deal.

Shotcrete. Shotcrete is the generic term for several systems of blowing concrete through hoses in order to eliminate most forms entirely. The dry concrete mixture and water are piped separately to the nozzle. The mix occurs at the moment of expulsion from the nozzle. Since the concrete strikes the surface with considerable force, the system works best against an earth backing, as in a reservoir or swimming pool lining. Wire-mesh reinforcement may be formed into a structure with tough fabric backing to create freestanding buildings of shotcrete. Because the mix is dry and the concrete very dense from impact, if properly cured, shotcrete can be a very high quality concrete, attaining a working stress of 9,000 psi or more.

Precast Concrete. The ultimate in reuse of forms is precast concrete. Highly finished forms, often of stainless steel, can be reused thousands of times, with the last casting virtually identical to the first. Precast concrete has a long history. Originally it was used to take advantage of its resemblance to limestone to make "cast stone" lintels, sills, and any other architectural details associated with stone. Indeed, it is often difficult to tell this product from quarried stone. While still available in this form, precast concrete is also utilized for many newer products.

Perhaps the greatest ingenuity has been used to produce curtain-wall units. If there is a sufficient number of units in a building, forms can be custom made exclusively for the job. If the work is begun near the start of construction, hundreds of units can be fabricated, with the help of steam curing, by the time installation is required. These products can be very precise, with all necessary fittings incorporated for installation. Concrete has fewer problems with expansion and contraction than other curtain-wall materials.

Precast structural members, often prestressed, are also commonly available in a great variety of types, including I beams, T beams, double T beams, and a number of different floor-slab systems. The high-quality reusable forms and the shop conditions at all stages of the process assure a much more reliable product than field conditions can permit. The main disadvantage with precasting is the transportation, lifting, and placing of great weight. The latter is dealt with by modern handling equipment, the former is a greater or lesser problem according to the distance the structures are to be transported.

PRECAST CONCRETE SHAPES

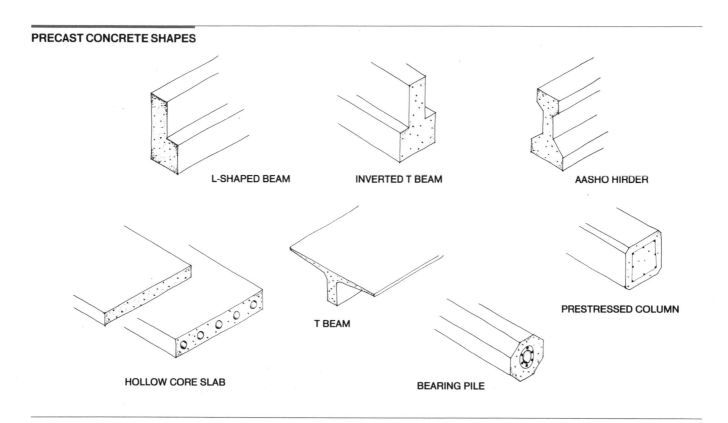

L-SHAPED BEAM

INVERTED T BEAM

AASHO HIRDER

HOLLOW CORE SLAB

T BEAM

BEARING PILE

PRESTRESSED COLUMN

Ferro Cemento. The Italian engineer/architect Pier Luigi Nervi seemed to have had an almost mystical understanding of concrete reinforcement. Believing that concrete was strongest close to the steel, he substituted a fine mesh of steel for the few large rods customarily used. The concrete had to be of fine aggregate only, and applied by trowel. Whatever the theory, Nervi produced many remarkable structures, such as the Palace of Sport in Rome, by this system, which he called *ferro cemento*. This theory led to the development of thin-shell concrete, where the curving shapes create sound structure with remarkable economy. The epitome of thin-shell concrete is the cosmic radiation laboratory at the University of Mexico, designed by the Spanish-born architect Felix Candela.

Prestressing and Post-tensioning. A rather recent structural innovation has been the process of using tensioned steel cables in concrete beams and slabs to lower the neutral axis in the concrete. This puts more of the concrete in compression; it has the same effect as deepening the beam or slab. Greater spans with shallower members become possible. Prestressing becomes part of the process of precasting. The cables are placed in the forms, then one end is anchored and the other subjected to a measured tension with hydraulic jacks. The concrete is placed and cured, after which the cables are released. The subsequent compression of the concrete causes the member to rise slightly in the center. This camber should flatten when the member is installed in the structure. This not only improves the spanning capability but also reduces deflection, or sagging, of the spanning member.

Post-tensioning is for members too large to build in the yard or to transport to the site, such as large bridge spans. In this system, formwork is built in the usual manner, and conduit for the cables is laid in the forms. After the concrete is placed and cured, the cables are pulled through the conduits, locked at one end, and fastened to hydraulic jacks at the other. After the appropriate tension is applied, the jack ends of the cables are locked and the formwork can be removed.

The difference between the two systems is a matter of scale and convenience in the work; the structural principals are the same.

Bonding Agents. New concrete will bond well to freshly set concrete, but no useful bond can be expected to occur with old work. For this purpose, bonding agents have been devised. Since these are proprietary products, the manufacturer's instructions must be followed. Typically they are painted on the old surface and create adhesion between the old and new materials. These products are reliable and allow successful repair of old concrete, even to the feathering of the edge of a ramp.

Finishing. The plastic nature of concrete is the basis for most concrete finishing. The surface of the concrete becomes the reverse image of the form. Where the concrete is to be left exposed, great care and even greater ingenuity are often exercised to produce the desired texture or pattern in the concrete. Le Corbusier first created the system of using many narrow, rough boards for formwork as at the Unité d'Habitation at Marseilles, which is virtually all concrete. These boards were probably all that were available in postwar France, but they suited his style very well, adapting to curved surfaces and lending interesting texture. With the increased use of plywood, the new brutalists of the sixties reveled in the lightly grained surfaces with obvious joints at the module of the plywood sheet. Since then many other systems have been developed for the modification of forms to create textures in the concrete. New textures from the formwork continue to challenge architects and designers.

Taking note of the fact that concrete is artificial stone, most of the finishes suitable to stone can be imposed on concrete. The most popular have been bush hammering and sandblasting. The former leaves its characteristic pattern, the latter leaves something like a honed finish. If the coarse aggregate is very hard, it will be prominently exposed.

Solid concrete alone does not make a very satisfactory exterior wall material. While inherently waterproof, with shrinkage it develops many hairline cracks that will permit water seepage. Treatment with sealants will help but seldom completely cure the problem. Stone concrete is a very poor insulation; lightweight concrete is somewhat better.

Concrete takes paint well, particularly cement-based paint. This bonds with concrete to make a virtually permanent finish. While still fresh, concrete may be easily cement plastered. With fully cured concrete it is advisable to first use a bonding agent.

Cement finish is the simplest form of finish for a concrete slab. When partly set, the surface is dusted with pure portland cement to absorb excess water and harden the surface. The surface is then troweled and, as curing proceeds, the steel trowel polishes the surface. Power equipment is available for this work for larger scale projects. Pigments may be added to the finishing cement if color is desired. Hardening agents are available for floors that must take greater than average wear.

Various textures may be used to provide a nonslip surface for steps, ramps, and exterior walks. The simplest is that created by brushing the partially set surface with a stiff broom. Various textures can be impressed upon fresh concrete, when desired. Metal grids can be fabricated from welded strap iron to press a pattern that may simulate many masonry surfaces, such as cobblestone or brick. With greater integrity the designer's imagination is the only limit to nonimitative patterns. As with any cement finish, color can be introduced. While the slab is fresh, mixes of special concretes may be placed on it as a topping. If the slab has cured too long, it may be necessary to apply a bonding agent before the topping. These toppings may be of any thickness, but ½″ to 1″ (13 to 25 mm) are most common. Toppings permit great control over the finish surface. It is difficult to be precise with coloring agents, for instance, with the dusting process; mechanically mixing a topping will give more assured results. Special aggregates such as marble chips and river pebbles can be used. A retarder may be brushed on the surface to permit the surface cement to be washed away, exposing the aggregate.

Terrazzo is the Italian word for terrace, but modern terrazzo is a special kind of concrete topping, often very ornamental. In the manufacture of terrazzo, a bed of rather dry mortar is spread over the slab and leveled to about a 1″ (25 mm) thickness. A prepared grid of brass or zinc strips is pressed into the mortar; these project about ¾″ (19 mm). This grid is filled with a special concrete mix of white cement and marble chips. Any pigment may be used, if desired, and any combination of color or size of marble chips. After curing overnight, the topping is ground smooth and polished with special equipment, then sealed. Although used a great deal in residential floors in parts of the country where slab-on-grade construction is common, terrazzo is mostly associated with monumental buildings. The grid, which is primarily installed to create control joints, may be fabricated in ornamental designs. The various spaces in the pattern may be filled with different colors, giving much latitude to the designer.

Concrete in Interiors

Concrete, with the exception of flooring, must be viewed as primarily a structural material, not one that can reasonably be used for new interior partitions. It may seem, therefore, to be a material that is not associated with interior design. It is, however, a material much in evidence in twentieth-century buildings, and a material that designers must understand and handle. Concrete interior surfaces cannot present the softness of fabrics or the warmth of wood, but this does not mean that exposed concrete is necessarily objectionable in aesthetic terms. The honesty of expression of concrete, as with other structural materials, is often much appreciated by designers. This is less the case with the general public, and it may become the task of the designer to convince a client that an interior concrete surface is perfectly acceptable.

The patterned surfaces created on concrete by the formwork, most often the wood grain of plywood sheets, provide the main visual interest. The standard 4′ × 8′ (1.2 × 2.4 m) sheet size will create a modular expression on exposed walls. Since concrete takes paint very well, the designer can choose between leaving the surface in its natural state or painting it. If viewed as unsatisfactory, concrete can be plastered, paneled, or receive any of the other interior treatments available. The concrete surface should be treated with dampproofing if the finish material is in any way susceptible to water damage.

Small interior spaces that are entirely surfaced in concrete will feel heavy and cell-like. However, most concrete buildings have structural exterior walls with nonstructural interior partitions, usually finished by drywall system. In most spaces, only one wall remains as exposed concrete to create an accent wall within the individual space. Columns may also express the patterns left by the formwork. Cylindrical columns are usually formed with paper tubing that leaves an interesting spiral texture.

To experience the extreme to which concrete has been carried as an interior finish, one must visit the house built by Dr. Mercer in Buck's County, Pennsylvania. Mercer, an eccentric physician and an avid collector, designed a house for himself that was not only all concrete, but even had concrete door casings and drawer frames. The plastic flexibility of concrete allows almost any shapes to be formed, despite all conventions, rules, and logic.

9 Plaster and Drywall

Gypsum is the popular name for hydrous calcium sulphate, a natural mineral that easily gains or loses its hydration, changing from powder to crystal. Gypsum is used for making plaster, wallboard, and other construction products.

Building lime is calcium hydrate, often mixed with magnesium hydrate. Used to make the original plaster, lime is principally used today as an additive to gypsum or to make a special finish coat.

Plaster is a pasty composition of gypsum (or lime or portland cement) with sand and water, which hardens and is used to cover walls and ceilings.

Gypsum board is a prepared panel of extruded gypsum paste with paper surfaces. Often called "sheet rock," it is available in several thicknesses, most commonly ½" (13 mm). Like most sheet building materials, the standard size is 4' × 8' (1.2 × 2.4 m), but it can be obtained in larger sizes as well.

Drywall is a wall and ceiling covering system using sheets of gypsum board, with the joints and fasteners taped and filled. The finished product resembles plaster.

From earliest times walls of stone and wattle (woven twigs) were plastered with mud from the earth around the building to produce a smooth and wind-tight wall. At some time in prehistory, in the Mediterranean region, the deliberate development of materials for high-quality plaster occurred. A slow-setting but very durable plaster was created by mixing lime with clean sand. This became the material of choice for some of the most famous walls and ceilings of history, including the murals of Pompeii and the ceiling of the Sistine Chapel. In the late Middle Ages, gypsum was introduced to Europe, probably by the Spanish Moors, who certainly used it most expertly. While not highly resistant to water and, therefore, suitable only for interiors, gypsum plaster's quick setting time and precise moldability made possible fast construction and highly ornamental work. The invention of portland cement yielded a quick-setting plaster that was completely water resistant and suitable for exterior use. This became a favorite surface for Modern architects of the thirties because of the smooth plane surfaces it made possible.

Any building constructed up to the 1950s is likely to have plaster interior finish. Gypsum board began to appear about that time and rapidly displaced plaster as the most common interior surface, as the drywall system requires less skill to assemble and is less expensive to install.

Properties of Plaster
To create building lime, limestone is heated to a temperature high enough to drive carbon dioxide from the compound. The resultant product is quicklime, or calcium oxide. Some limestones contain a greater or lesser amount of magnesium, as does the resultant product; this functions much the same as the calcium. When quicklime is added to water, a very strong chemical reaction occurs releasing heat. Some of the water joins the compound as the hydroxyl radical, releasing hydrogen gas. The end product is slaked lime, also known as hydrated lime or calcium hydroxide. This will be a paste from the excess water, but is dried into a powder for shipping.

To make plaster, the slaked lime is mixed with two or three parts sand and sufficient water to make a paste. After application the water evaporates and the lime begins to absorb carbon dioxide from the air. This chemically binds with the lime, forming limestone again. The curing process is slow, requiring a week or more between coats. Magnesium hydroxide requires even more time to cure, so the ratio of calcium to magnesium determines a relatively fast or slow curing time. (Because the absorption of carbon dioxide is a slow process, the fresco painters did not have to hurry their work as much as is popularly believed.) The end product is a most durable surfacing, suitable for interior or exterior use. Attesting to this are the murals uncovered from the volcanic ash of Vesuvius after almost two thousand years of exposure. But modern patience is short and, for interiors at least, lime has yielded entirely to gypsum, except as an additive. The other exception is the use of lime putty as a water-resistant finish coat.

Gypsum is a widely distributed mineral found in various forms, all of which are chemically hydrous calcium sulphate. In a pure state, gypsum may be found as the translucent marblelike alabaster. A large, exceptionally pure deposit of gypsum lies beneath the city of Paris, giving us the term for pure white powdered gypsum: "plaster of Paris." In this form the plaster sets so rapidly that it can only be used for casting. Additives had to be found to slow the setting time of gypsum enough for use as a wall and ceiling surfacing material. Mined gypsum is in its hydrate state. To become usable the crystalline form must be heated to about 250 to 300 degrees Fahrenheit (120 to 150 degrees Celsius). At this temperature about three quarters of the water is driven from the compound, leaving a hemihydrate. This is the form in which gypsum is used by the building trades. In normal use, gypsum hemihydrate is mixed with fine aggregate and water to make a stiff paste. Curing represents a rehydration back to the original hydrate, which adheres to the aggregate in the mixture as well as the backing.

Gypsum plaster is a durable material if it is not wet too frequently. Most causes of early damage can be attributed to water leakage. After a long period of time, perhaps a hundred years, the cementing power of gypsum breaks down. At this time the plaster reverts to a powdery sand. The condition is not always immediately apparent because multiple coats of paint may hold the surface together. Piercing the surface, however, produces a stream of fine granules. Another symptom of decay is what appears to be peeling paint, but in fact is the finish plaster coat peeling. When this condition occurs nothing can be done to revitalize the plaster. It must be stripped off and replaced. This is clearly a major project, and the option may be chosen to cover the old plaster with new material fastened through the old plaster to the lath or framing members. Drywall will simulate the old plaster surface and is often the most economical solution.

Because of the water bound into its molecular structure, gypsum is inherently very highly fire-resistant. Because of the low temperature required for dehydration, gypsum is a relatively energy-efficient material. When other considerations are added—rapid curing, relative ease of molding and shaping, low cost—it is clear why gypsum has replaced lime for interior surfacing.

The manufacture and chemistry of portland cement is reviewed in the chapter on concrete. Used for exterior surfaces, the mixture of cement, fine aggregate, and water must be cured like concrete to reach its maximum strength. Thereafter is should be completely weather-resistant except for the hairline cracks that inevitably form due to shrinkage. Any plaster used for exterior work is often called "stucco," an Italian word for plaster.

Acoustical Plaster. Gypsum mixed with two to three parts of expanded mica makes a fine, acoustically absorbent surface. The base coats are troweled on, but the finish is sprayed on to create a pebbly surface that enhances the acoustical properties of the plaster. Expanded mica is a rather fragile material, easily brushed from the surface. For this reason acoustical plaster is not suitable for walls or low ceilings. For a time, asbestos fibers were added to the mix for reinforcement, but since the dangers of asbestos have become known, this practice has been discontinued. There are still buildings with asbestos plaster; in most communities these surfaces are being covered or removed.

Finishing Plaster. Fresh plaster is rather strongly alkaline, which diminishes as the curing process proceeds. This "hot" plaster can affect paint color in oil-based paints. To hurry the process of neutralization, plaster walls can be brushed with mild acid, such as vinegar. Latex paints are not affected by mild alkalinity, so they present no problem. Plaster makes an excellent base for almost any other kind of finish: wallpaper, vinyl coverings, cloth, tile, and so forth. Under tile, or in other locations that are expected to be wet, cement plaster should be used.

Plaster in Construction

Plaster of all kinds must be applied to some surface, either masonry or lath, to which it can mechanically adhere. The surfaces must be prepared with grounds and the plaster applied in several coats. Since lime plaster has virtually disappeared in modern construction, the following process is for gypsum plaster, with some references to cement plaster.

Plaster may be applied directly to masonry walls. For interior walls and ceilings of wood-frame buildings in the eighteenth century, the original lath was wood. Roughsawn lumber about ⅜″ by 1⅜″ (10 mm × 35 mm), invariably 4 foot long (1.2 m), was the standard lath. This set the building module still very much in use today. Studs 16″ (400 mm) on center allow four nailing points per lath. The laths are started on consecutive studs to distribute the vertical joints. Spacing the laths about ⅜″ (10 mm) apart allows the first coat of plaster to be keyed into these spaces. Wood lath is still found in any building dating back to the early decades of this century, after which metal lath began to appear.

In the beginning, sheet metal was perforated to key the plaster and then nailed to the surfaces to be plastered. The introduction of metal was to improve the fire-resistance of a building and to reduce the installation labor. A method of punching sheet metal so that it could be drawn out to several times its original width led to modern expanded metal lath. This material proved more economical than wood lath in material and installation, and soon it eliminated wood lath entirely. Also available is ribbed expanded metal lath, which has an improved ability to span studs or joists. Another type of metal lath is made from welded wire mesh, usually with a paper backing, for the adhesion and reinforcement of cement plaster.

With the development of gypsum board, an even more economical lathing system became apparent. Sheets of the board were nailed up as lath and two (rather than the usual three) coats of plaster were used to arrive at the same thickness as plaster on wood or metal lath. This system began to eclipse metal lath in the late 1950s, just about the time that gypsum board began to replace plastering altogether with the drywall system.

The first coat of plaster, called the "scratch" coat, is a mixture of one part gypsum to two or three parts sand. This paste is troweled on rather thinly, but with enough force to press the plaster into the lath to key it well. While still wet, this coat is scratched to improve the adhesion of the next coat.

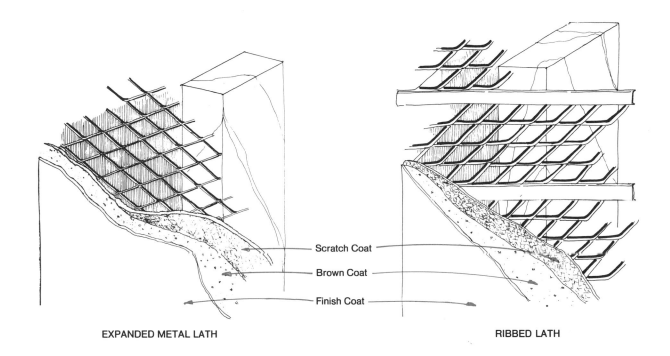

Scratch Coat

Brown Coat

Finish Coat

EXPANDED METAL LATH

RIBBED LATH

Grounds are set up to establish the proper finish level of the walls and ceiling. These are strips of wood shimmed and nailed to the top and bottom of the walls; sometimes door and window frames also serve as plaster grounds. The grounds are left exposed when the plastering is completed, but are traditionally covered by baseboards and moldings in the finish work, which posed a challenge to Modern designers who wished to eliminate moldings.

The second coat, called the "hair" or "brown" coat, represents the bulk of the thickness of the surface finish, about ¾″ (19 mm). This mixture is similar to the first coat, with a percentage of fiber added. Originally this fiber was cow hair, hence the name. Now, more often, synthetic fibers are substituted. The term "brown" comes from the color of the lower grade gypsum used for undercoating. With the grounds as a guide, by means of a "darby," a straightedge long enough to reach between the grounds, the effective finish thickness is applied. This coat may require several days to dry, depending upon the temperature, the atmospheric humidity, and the ventilation of the space.

When gypsum lath is used, the number of coats is reduced to two. Plaster adheres strongly to the paper coating of gypsum lath, eliminating the need for the scratch coat. Since the lath is ⅜″ (10 mm) thick, the first coat is also about ⅜″ (10 mm) thick. The finish coat is executed in the same manner as plaster on metal lath.

The finish coat is very thin, perhaps between 1/16″ and ⅛″ (1.5 to 3 mm). The materials used vary according to the desired finish and the requirements of the space. For normal conditions, with a smooth finish, a fine gypsum mix is applied and smoothed with a steel trowel. After partial setting, the surface is polished with the trowel. If a slightly rough finish is preferred, a small amount of coarse sand is added, and the polishing is omitted. Where areas of high moisture are encountered, lime putty may be used, resulting in a hard, highly polished, water-resistant surface. For the same conditions Keen's cement may also be used. A mixture of very pure completely dehydrated gypsum and lime putty, Keen's cement will take a high polish and will be water-resistant; however, it has a more rapid setting time than lime putty.

Any number of textures are possible with the finish coat, depending upon the ingenuity of the plasterer. A wood float may be used, which sticks to the plaster and raises a characteristic texture. This texture may, in turn, be partially smoothed with a steel trowel, leaving an "orange peel" finish. The plaster may be deliberately applied unevenly to leave a coarse "Spanish" texture. The finish may be applied by dashing it on with a broom, creating a very rough finish. The trowel can be rotated, or moved in many swirling patterns. Most patterns were devised to simulate the finishes for some eclectic style of architecture, so modern designers tend to settle for smooth- or sand-finish plaster.

Ornament. Plaster can be shaped into highly ornamental forms, as any number of baroque churches can attest. Any shape that lath can be formed into can be plastered. Until recently "run" moldings of plaster were a common decoration. Run moldings are created by drawing metal templates of the proper profile along freshly applied plaster. The last building in the United States to have a run plaster ceiling was the Metropolitan Opera in New York City. When no plasterers could be found with the necessary skills, some old men were recruited from retirement to complete the work. Run plaster is indeed a dying art.

Precast ornament has been with us for a long time: the Moorish work of the Alhambra at Granada, Spain dates from the fourteenth century. This work clearly is the culmination of a long tradition. Firms specializing in cast-plaster ornament still exist from a period when the skills of the plasterers had degenerated to a few stock designs.

If ornamental work is to be restored, there is a fairly simple process: an undamaged area is selected and latex molds are made, from which as many copies as required can be cast. These are cemented in place and the joints filled.

Properties of Drywall

Since the introduction of this system, with its very substantial economies, drywall has largely replaced plaster. A sheet of gypsum paste is extruded 4′ (1.2 m) wide of the desired thickness. The mix includes some paper fiber for reinforcement and some foaming agent for lightness. As the gypsum mixture is extruded, paper sheets are automatically applied to the surfaces and wrapped around the edges. The surface to be exposed is of higher quality paper, ready for paint; the edges are tapered to facilitate finishing. The sheets are cut, usually to 8' (2.4 m), but lengths of 10', 12', and 16' (3, 3.66, and 4.88 m) are available. Thickness may vary from ¼" to 1" (6 to 25 mm), with ⅜" and ½" (10 and 13 mm) predominating. Long sheets are used to minimize joints. The proper thickness to use depends on a number of factors: the span of the studs or joists, the degree of fire-resistance required, the sound-reduction desired, and the problems of weight. The latter is of special concern for ceilings.

For high-moisture areas—kitchens, baths, and the like—a more highly water-resistant board is produced. Asphaltic compounds are added to the gypsum, and an underwrapping of water-resistant paper is included. The surface paper is tinted green and the back of the sheets are stamped "WR" for identification. While more water-resistant than ordinary gypsum board, this treated board is not, by any means, suitable for steam rooms or saunas. However, it may be used as a base for tile in a tub surround, if a coating of waterproof cement is first applied.

Type "X" gypsum board, a board with a denser gypsum core, is used especially for fire-resistance. It is reinforced with fiberglass and has fire-retardant additives. This board may be stamped "type X" or "FR" on the back, for identification. The most popular thickness is ⅝" (16 mm), since this is rated as one-hour fire-resistance.

Foil-backed gypsum board has aluminum foil in place of paper backing. The foil creates an excellent vapor barrier, and if an air space of at least ¾" (19 mm) is left behind the board, the reflective aluminum surface has a considerable thermal insulation value.

Predecorated gypsum board has a vinyl covering, available in endless textures and colors, wrapped across the face and around the edges of the board. This is meant to be a finished surface upon installation. A quick and easy wall-finish solution, these boards present the joys and tribulations of any vinyl surfacing. There is the added discipline of an obvious modular joint. Some boards are provided with extra vinyl flaps to be cemented over the joints to reduce this problem.

Drywall in Construction

Gypsum board is nailed to wood studs and joists about 16" (.4 m) in both directions. The nails are either blued steel or tempered aluminum to prevent rust. Needle-sharp points, ringed shanks, and large heads minimize nail "popping." The hammer should drive the head below the surface enough to leave a dimple without breaking the paper. An alternative is electrically driven screws, automatically set to the correct depth. For sheet metal studs, the screws are self-drilling and self-tapping.

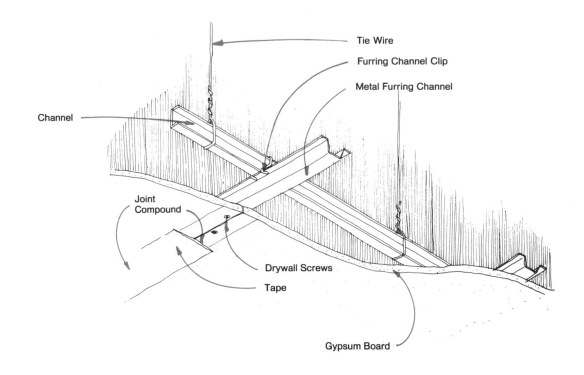

Tie Wire

Furring Channel Clip

Metal Furring Channel

Channel

Joint Compound

Drywall Screws

Tape

Gypsum Board

Ceilings, especially in commercial work, are often suspended. This lowers the ceiling height, when desired, and eases the distribution of mechanical equipment. The usual system is to secure wires to the structural ceiling, which support a grid of steel channels. The gypsum board is screwed to these channels.

Gypsum board is also glued to wall supports with a panel cement extruded from caulking guns. More often this is used when double layering is done for increased fire- or sound-resistance.

Openings must be cut for doors and windows, of course, but also for all electrical penetrations: outlets, switches, light fixtures. Gypsum board is very brittle and not suited to curves except of large radius. With a little judicious wetting, tighter curves can be bent. As a general rule, however, plastic forms are not in the nature of the material.

After the board is installed, corner beads are fastened to all outside corners to minimize joints. The space is readied for finishing.

Taping the joints and filling the nail or screw depressions is a multistage operation. Joint compound, composed of fully hydrated gypsum in a paste form, is troweled over all joints and fasteners. Paper or fiberglass reinforcing tape is then pressed into the compound over the joints and folded into the inside corners. The compound is smoothed and allowed to dry. A second coat is necessary to cover well and to feather the edges perhaps 6″ to 12″ (150 to 300 mm) from the joint or fastener. Because the compound shrinks when drying, a third coat is often necessary. Finally the work is smoothed by sanding, which is often

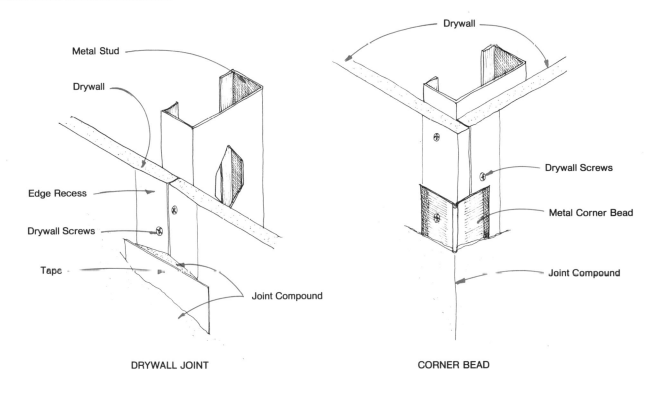

Metal Stud

Drywall

Edge Recess

Drywall Screws

Tape

Joint Compound

DRYWALL JOINT

Drywall

Drywall Screws

Metal Corner Bead

Joint Compound

CORNER BEAD

done wet to reduce dust. If the work is done well, the sanding will be minimal. The compound is not waterproof, so the surfaces may be polished with a damp sponge. All this work can be done with a few simple tools, but elaborate devices have been invented to speed the work for the professional. The greatest innovation is self-adhering open-web fiberglass tape. This is applied before the compound, which then penetrates the openings. Unlike paper tape, fiberglass tape is dimensionally stable and will not trap air to form bubbles.

If a smooth finish is desired, the space is ready for paint. Any of the textures available for plaster can be applied to drywall since plaster adheres to the paper and joint compound very well. Most often texture is applied by thinning some compound and rolling it on with a paint roller. The texture will conceal less-than-perfect walls and joints. After a day or two of drying, the surfaces are ready for paint.

Fire Protection and Acoustics. The treatment of gypsum board for fire-protection and sound-penetration is similar. The material is inherently good for both, and it is only a question of how many layers to apply to generate so many hours of fire-resistance or decibels of sound-reduction. The greatest care must be taken with the joints. They should be filled well before taping and, if multiple-layered, should be well lapped. The most neglected weak points are at the head and the base. Leakage here will spoil the effectiveness of the wall for both fire and sound. They should be tightly fitted and well caulked.

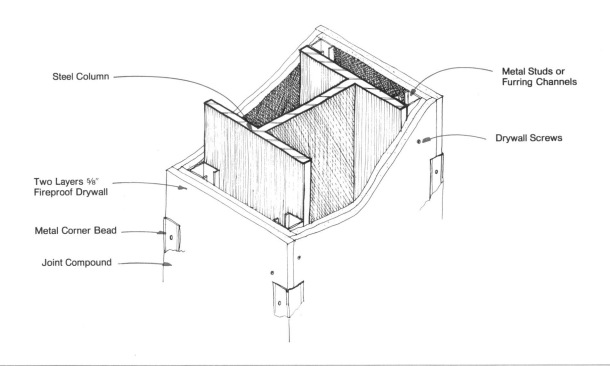

Steel Column

Metal Studs or Furring Channels

Drywall Screws

Two Layers ⅝" Fireproof Drywall

Metal Corner Bead

Joint Compound

Plaster is clearly superior to drywall. With greater thickness and density and with the assured absence of any gaps or holes, the sound-transmission and fire-resistance of plaster is greatly superior to those of an ordinary drywall finish. With the surface brought to true by grounds, rather than directly fastened to supporting members, plaster will produce a straighter wall. Plaster can be made to conform to any shape and, in the hands of a skilled artisan, to any degree of ornamentation. True as all this may be, drywall has the overwhelming advantage of lower cost. In the competitive market of today, this price advantage is leading the ancient trade of the plasterer into extinction. Many limitations of drywall can be overcome. Fire and acoustics are managed by layering and care in installation. The use of sheet metal studs eliminates the warpage of wood, leading to truer walls. The demand for plastic form and ornamentation has nearly vanished over the decades of domination of building by Modern architects. Only the revival of plastic shapes and the desire for ornamentation could bring plaster close to its former eminence.

Plaster and Drywall in Interiors

Eighteenth-century interiors such as those created by the Adam brothers used plaster in a superbly artistic way. Delicate ornamentation was applied to walls and ceilings by highly skilled craftsmen. While plastering is a dying art, in recent years the fashion involving classical details and ornamentalism has rekindled some interest in this craft.

During the Victorian era and into this century, plaster was also used in furnishings, such as wall consoles, and elaborate chandeliers. Completely pliable when fresh, plaster lends itself to every possible decorative shape. However, because it is brittle and easily damaged, plaster never achieved widespread use as a component of movable furniture.

In recent years, gypsum board has become the most widely used interior surface in residential and nonresidential interiors. Although practically indistinguishable from a simple plaster surface, gypsum board never has the soundness or quality of plaster. A plaster wall created by a good craftsperson can be a remarkably level and plumb surface. Gypsum board walls can only be as level as the studs behind. It takes a top-notch carpenter as well as a good drywaller to produce a straight and true wall.

Plaster and drywall are usually painted, although they take any finish material very well. The use of gypsum board for ceilings is rather more difficult, given the weight of the material. In inexpensive commercial construction, a suspended ceiling of fiberboard panels with exposed splines is often used. This is never a first-rate solution and proclaims the cheapest work.

Despite the simplicity of drywall construction, it is quite satisfactory for most purposes. One weakness is drywall's inability to support anything between the studs; even picture hooks may pull out quite easily. Consequently, anything to be hung from the wall must have advance preparation. Wood or metal studs or cross members must be installed to receive the nails or screws. Old-fashioned plaster could not support a great deal of weight, but at least it had enough body to support pictures.

The regret articulated about the loss of the art of plastering, with its flexibility of form, is not to deny the remarkable work done in gypsum board. Drywall is an ingenious invention that has greatly reduced the cost of building.

10 Glass and Plastics

Glass and plastics are associated in building construction because certain plastics are often used for glazing. In fact, both are put to other uses as well, especially plastics.

Glass is an amorphous, inorganic, translucent noncrystalline substance, composed largely of silica, sodium oxide, and calcium oxide. In building, glass is principally used to make weather-tight windows.

Plastic is defined as any material without natural structure capable of being formed and molded and then retaining that shape. In modern usage plastic usually means a synthetic organic compound, made mostly from petrochemicals.

Caulking is a substance or process for sealing leaks in cracks and joints. Traditionally composed of whiting (calcium carbonate) and linseed oil, now caulking is usually prepared from organic compounds—any compound containing the amorphous element carbon, often in highly complex structure.

Adhesives are any products used to join parts. Once primarily derived from animal hides, now most adhesives are synthetic organic compounds.

Glass

Glass is found in nature as a black volcanic product called obsidian, which was highly desired by Stone Age cultures for tools and weapon points. Glass is also found, more rarely, as fulgurites: slender glass tubes created when lighting strikes an appropriate raw material. The earliest glass was manufactured in Egypt and Mesopotamia about 1500 B.C., probably as a by-product of the growing interest in reducing metals from minerals. The ancient Egyptians valued glass as a precious stone, setting both natural stones and glass in the gold ornaments found in the tomb of Tutankhamen. The blowpipe appeared in about 30 B.C. when it was used to produce small glass vials for precious liquids. The Romans were producing window glass, rarely, by 50 B.C. If their windows were glazed at all, alabaster and agate were more often used.

In the centuries following, glassblowing was raised to a high art. Window panes were also produced by this technique. A large glass bubble was blown and rolled on a flat surface to form a cylinder. While still sufficiently plastic, the ends were cut off and the cylinder cut open and flattened. These relatively small sheets produced the small paned windows that were universal until the nineteenth century. The circular cut-off ends were sometimes leaded together, creating bull's-eye windows.

Small amounts of copper and iron salts almost universally present in the raw materials gave rise to the common "bottle green" glass. The introduction of other minerals produced glass of many colors, bringing about the art of stained glass in the eleventh century. This art reached its epitome with the windows created for the Medieval cathedrals.

The first plate glass was produced in France in 1688, but mass production of glass did not begin until the early twentieth century. A method of drawing a continuous sheet of glass from a vat was invented by Emile Fourcault, a Belgian, in 1902. Soon plate glass was available for mirrors and other more optically demanding uses. The most recent improvement in glass manufacture came in the 1960s with the float process, in which sheet glass can be made as fine as plate.

Glass can be made from pure silica, and is so made for laboratory glassware. It does, however, require high temperature to melt, 3,100 degrees Fahrenheit (1,700 degrees Celsius), and is difficult to work. The addition of sodium and calcium by about the volume of 15 percent and 10 percent respectively, lowers the melting point and improves the workability of the silica without hurting its optical qualities. There are many other formulas for producing glass with different qualities, but they are not at this time important to the building industry.

After the fusion of the base materials in a high-temperature furnace, the molten material is drawn into a sheet. This product must be cooled under controlled conditions so that it passes into the solid state without crystallization. This peculiar event gives glass some of the properties of a liquid, despite its solid state.

The first process for mass production of sheet glass was the Fourcault. With many improvements, it is still in use today. From a continuously fed furnace, a continuous sheet is drawn vertically from a pool of molten glass. A later improvement bends the sheet onto a flat bed of rollers to pass through a horizontal oven called a lehr. This process is called flame polishing, and helps flatten and smooth the glass. As the glass travels through the lehr it is slowly cooled, an annealing process. The sheets are next cut and stacked as a finished product called sheet or window glass. This is the lowest grade of glass, suitable for less critical uses.

Plate glass is pulled as a thicker sheet and passes through textured rollers to assure uniform thickness. The cut sheets are then passed through grinding and polishing beds, which assure parallel faces as well as a highly polished and transparent surface. Plate glass is the highest quality sheet glass and is used for mirrors and show windows. Mies van der Rohe liked the coarse pattern of unpolished plate and used it wherever he wanted obscure glass.

Float glass is a recent innovation that introduces a pond of molten tin before the glass enters the lehr. The heat of the molten tin keeps the glass soft while the high surface tension of the tin flattens it. The glass then passes through the lehr for annealing. The end product is close to plate glass in optical quality, but the cost is closer to that of sheet glass. Float glass is now being substituted for plate glass in many applications.

FLOAT GLASS PROCESS

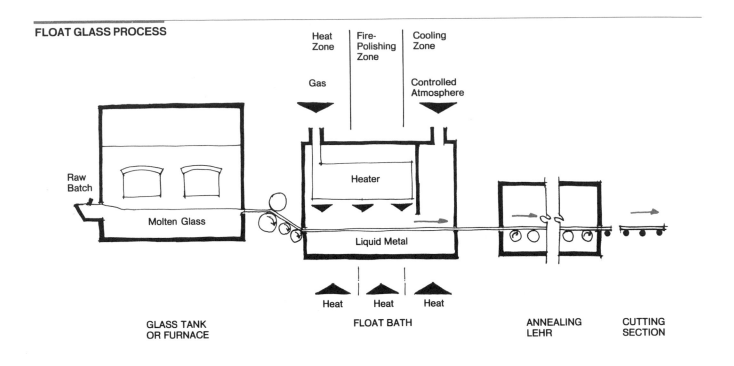

Sheet glass is used primarily for glazing small windows and can be somewhat wavy and optically imperfect. It is available in thicknesses of SS (single strength) at ³⁄₃₂″ (2.4 mm) to DS (double strength) at ⅛″ (3 mm). Heavy sheet may be ³⁄₁₆″ or ⁷⁄₃₂″ (4.8 and 5.6 mm) thick. Each thickness has a maximum size of glass area recommended. All thicknesses are selected for quality according to the degree of imperfection: AA, A, B.

Polished plate glass is inspected for imperfections, which are marked, and the sheets are cut so that the obvious flaws are excluded. Plate is used for glazing where the highest optical quality is required. Normal thicknesses are ⅛″ and ¼″ (3 and 6 mm). Heavy plate is available from ⁵⁄₁₆″ to ⅞″ (8 to 22 mm) and thicker for special purposes. The normal quality for all polished plate glass is "glazing." For ⅛″ and ¼″ thicknesses there are two extra grades: "mirror-glazing" and the top grade, "silvering."

Float glass is manufactured in the same range of thicknesses and qualities as polished plate glass. In fact, float glass is rapidly replacing the much more expensive polished plate and is becoming the most commonly used glass of any manufacture.

Specialty Glass. Obscure glass is made to provide light without transparency. Such glass may be etched with hydrofluoric acid, or sandblasted, to eliminate optical transparency. This may be done on one or both sides depending on the degree of transparency loss desired. These processes cause some loss of strength in the sheet, which must be taken into consideration with the opening size.

Patterned glass resembles the preparation of plate glass. The still soft glass may be passed through steel rollers to emboss a pattern on one or both sides. These patterns vary widely from one manufacturer to another and to the degree of obscureness imposed. Some of the patterns are hammered, pebbled, ribbed, cobwebbed, and even flowered. In this category are also prismed patterns, which will deflect more of the light in a particular direction. This is sometimes useful for projecting a more even light into a space.

Welded wire mesh is inserted into a near-molten glass sheet to create wire glass. Most often the sheet is ¼" (6 mm) thick. The glass itself may be obscure or optically clear. Although the wire does reinforce the glass to some extent, its main function is to hold the glass together in the event of breakage. While this may resist forced entry to some degree, the principal purpose of the wire is to reduce the possibility of injury from scattered glass. Smoke or fire doors may also continue to function after the glass has broken. The Underwriter's Laboratory has established standards for the use of wire glass in fire protection. These standards should be consulted whenever appropriate.

Glass of any thickness, ⅛" (3 mm) or more, may be tempered, with the exceptions of wire glass and some deeply patterned glass. This process subjects the glass to high temperature followed by rapid cooling. The

---

PATTERNED, WIRE, AND LAMINATED GLASS

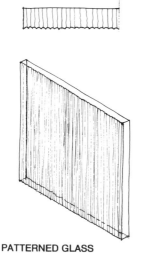

PATTERNED GLASS

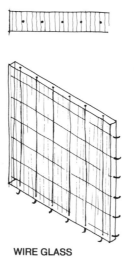

WIRE GLASS

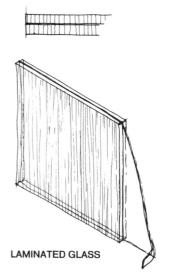

LAMINATED GLASS

surface tension of the sheet is greatly increased, thereby increasing the sheet's resistance to breaking by a factor of three to five times that of annealed glass. Some degree of deviation from flatness may be expected from the stresses, although this is true less so with thicker glass. Marks from the handling tongs maybe visible along one edge; these may be concealed if the glass is framed. If ultimately the glass is broken, it explodes into small cubic bits, which are much less likely to do harm than the great shards broken annealed glass becomes. Any glass that extends to the floor should be tempered, including all glazing for sliding glass doors. While tempering will permit the use of larger sizes of glass, its main purpose is safety.

A lesser degree of tempering results in what is called heat-strengthened glass. This product has about twice the strength of annealed glass. It is an economical option for when the qualities of fully tempered glass may not be required.

A certain number of stock sizes of tempered glass are maintained, especially for the requirements of standardized sliding glass doors. No glass can be cut, drilled, or otherwise altered after the tempering process. All such work must be done beforehand. This means that every piece of tempered glass for a project must be ordered directly from the plant in advance. Shop drawings may be necessary, according to the complexity of the work, and a lead time of six to eight weeks is the usual allowance.

Laminated glass was originally developed for the automotive industry. Sometimes called "safety glass," it has found uses in construction. The simplest form of laminated glass is a sandwich of two layers of glass with a layer of clear plastic cemented in between. If broken, the pieces of glass continue to adhere to the more flexible plastic sheet. For most applications, tempered glass has replaced laminate, but for certain uses laminated glass is still desirable. It has higher resistance to sound-penetration then solid glass; also, multiple-layered laminates can be used for protection from bullets and for such high-strength requirements as large aquariums.

Glass is very poor thermal insulation and water vapor in the air will frequently mist the windows in cold weather. To alleviate this problem, double-glazed insulating glass was devised. Double glazing alone will improve the insulation value of glass, but will not prevent misting. This is done by sealing the space between the sheets and replacing the entrapped air with super-dry air. This air cannot mist the cold outside glass. The seal is created by several patented methods. Small panes may have their edges fused; larger ones may be fitted with a rubber-gasketed aluminum channel. The overall thickness can range from ⅝" to 1" (16 to 25 mm). As with tempered glass, certain popular sizes may be in stock, such as the most common sizes used for standard sliding glass doors. Other sizes, and all shapes other than rectangular, must be ordered from the factory.

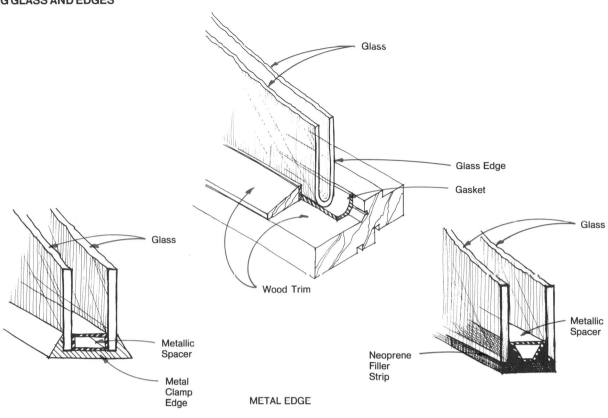

By including admixtures in the glassmaking process, various colors can be produced. Colors of every hue and chroma are created for use in stained glass, which is only a small part of the production of tinted glass. The largest part is for the reduction of light and heat transmission. Gray, bronze, green, and, more recently, blue are the most common colors used. Gray is the most popular tint because it causes no color distortion in the interiors. Bronze is very popular for cosmetic reasons. Tinted glass is a proprietary product and detailed specifications must be obtained from the manufacturers. In general, light and transmission may range from 80 percent down to 15 percent or less. Often the transmission of heat, in the form of infrared radiation, will vary widely. It should be realized that clear glass transmits only 90 percent of light.

Tints may also be added in the form of coatings fused to the surface in the float furnace. Plastic films with most of the qualities of color and reflectivity may be applied to glass after construction is completed.

Reflecting glass, sometimes called "one-way glass," is created by bonding a microscopically thin layer of metal to the glass surface. In sunlight this will reflect like a mirror, although from the interior the glass will be quite transparent. At night the process is reversed, making surfaces mirrored in the interior, transparent from the outside. The glass may be used for observation windows from room to room. It is important to remember that the observers must be at a lower light level than the observed for this to work.

Combinations of tinted, reflecting, and insulating glass are all possible. A certain caution must be heeded because of differential expansion that may occur between surfaces and sheets of insulating glass. Light and heat may be reflected from the surface, but some is absorbed. This absorbed energy will be changed to heat; glass, like all materials, must expand when heated. Care must be taken when selecting tints, surfacings, and the detailing of the framing to absorb expansion and contraction, and getting the advice of specialists may be advisable.

Quite apart from reflecting films used to create one-way glass, true mirrors are made by depositing a layer of pure silver on the back of the glass. The glass for fine mirrors is selected as noted above. After it is applied to the glass, the silver is given protective coatings to help prevent damage to its delicate surface. Care must be taken in installing mirrors to assure that the mounting surface will not damage the mirroring.

Opaque glass is sometimes called "structural glass" as opposed to window glass. Opacity is obtained by adding minerals in sufficient amounts to achieve the desired effect without preventing the vitrification process. Other opaque glass can be created by spraying minerals on the still hot surface. Opaque glass is used for spandrels or other surfaces where transparency is not desired.

The other principal use for glass in construction is in the form of fibers. Glass fibers are made by pressing molten glass through tiny orifices. The glass is then cooled and broken into long strands by air jets that jumble them into a woolly mass. This becomes a nonflammable thermal insulation. The wool is balled for bulk-filler use or extruded into batts and glued to a facing. Glass fibers are also used as reinforcement for many materials. They may be spun into yarn for woven reinforcement or woven into fire-resistant fabric.

Glass blocks are treated in Chapter 5 on unit masonry.

Plastics

The earliest plastics were developed in the nineteenth century of cellulose nitrate, commonly called celluloid. This was used to manufacture many objects previously made of natural materials such as horn, bone, and tortoiseshell. It brought about an explosion of cheaply produced goods. It was, also, so highly flammable as to be an explosive itself. Shortly after the turn of the century another, safer, moldable material was produced from phenolformaldehyde; it was known to the public as Bakelite. There continued to be a gradual development of synthetics up through the 1930s, when, as was so often the case, the demands of World War II spurred production. This was particularly true with synthetic rubber and silk (nylon).

A plastic, in modern terms, is an amorphous synthetic organic compound. A vast array of plastics has been developed, and more are coming along constantly. Most plastics are polymers, that is, composed of long chains of molecules. In the process called polymerization, small molecules link together into long chains. Some of the most popular plastics are given distinctive names, such as nylon, orlon, or vinyl; others have names such as polypropylene or polystyrene. Plastics appear everywhere: paints, fabrics, resilient flooring, hardware, piping, insulation, and so forth. This section is principally concerned with plastics for glazing, surfacing, and caulking and adhesives.

Polymethylmethacrylate, better known as acrylic, is the most common glazing material, except for glass. Most people are familiar with the material under the brand names of Lucite and Plexiglas. Acrylic glazings have excellent optical qualities and good resistance to weather and breakage. They are very light in weight, as little as one-seventh of the weight of glass of the same thickness. Acrylics take color additives well and, with careful heat application, can be bent or vacuum-formed. This makes possible the formation of the popular "bubble" skylights. The bad news is their lack of resistance to abrasion. Ordinary wear and tear will cause multiple surface scratching, which quickly degrades their optical quality. Acrylics with greater resistance to abrasion have been developed, at a greatly elevated price.

Polyester is so often reinforced with fiberglass that unsaturated polyester resins are commonly, but erroneously, called fiberglass. These resins are frequently made into thin sheets that are often corrugated or crimped for stiffness. Tough and weather resistant, fiberglass-reinforced polyester is translucent but not transparent. It is naturally honey-colored; however, pigments can be added to produce a range of colors and opacity. Fiberglass-reinforced polyester is widely used when natural light is desired, but a surface that can be seen through is not.

Polycarbonate, often called by the brand name Lexan, makes an optically good, exceptionally durable plastic glazing. Used where high-impact resistance is required, polycarbonate has many industrial applications and the greatest resistance to vandalism of any transparent substance so far devised.

Plastic Surfacing. Plastic laminate is composed of layers of kraft paper sandwiched with thermosetting plastic sheets. Plastic laminate is often called by the brand name Formica; however, there are many other manufacturers with their own brand names. The full process is to impregnate the kraft paper with phenolic resin. This resin is very adhesive and becomes very hard with good heat- and electrical resistance. The top layer is a decorative paper sheet covered with a layer of clear melamine resin. Melamine is very hard and scratch-resistant, and is not subject to most chemical attack. This sandwich is placed between polished steel plates and subjected to mild heat, 275 degrees Fahrenheit (135 degrees Celsius), and great pressure, 1,000 pounds per square foot. This thermosetting process unites the materials permanently. The back is scarified to improve adhesion. The material is produced in three grades: horizontal surfacing, vertical surfacing, and backing. The horizontal surfacing is thickest, at 0.05″ (1.3 mm). The vertical sheet is 0.03″ (0.8 mm), as is the backing, which has no decorative topping. The greater thickness will resist a heavier blow, but wear is dependent upon the surface layer, which is the same for both decorative grades. This thin laminate must be glued to a heavier backing, usually plywood or particle board. This may be done with a thermosetting adhesive in a shop or contact cement in the field. Because plastic laminate is very dimensionally stable and the backing material is not, warping due to differential expansion is likely. For this reason the other side of the fabrication should also receive a layer of laminate, backing grade if appearance is unimportant, to balance the stresses. A challenge to the designer is selecting the edge treatment required if the use of laminate is to be concealed.

PLASTIC LAMINATES

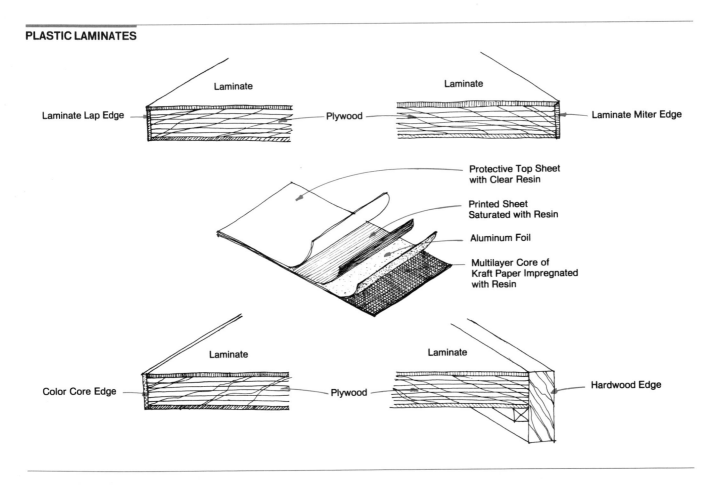

Until the 1950s, the decorative surface layer was often genuine wood veneer, but this did not hold up well at the joints. With laminates today, any wood appearance is by photographic process, as is any other natural-appearing material. Textures of any sort can be embossed on the pressure plates so that very realistic leather, cleft slate, and fabrics may be simulated. Smooth surfaces may be high gloss, semigloss, or matte.

A full range of samples from all the manufacturers will provide every color and pattern imaginable, and some unimaginable. Solid colors are at a premium because of the cleanliness required at every stage of manufacture.

There is a whole family of vinyl polymers used by the building industry. The most common and versatile is polyvinyl chloride (PVC). Among the products formed of PVC are sheet and tile flooring, gutters and downspouts, siding, window frames, piping, panel facings, and wallcoverings. (Some of these uses are discussed in other sections of this book.) While vinyls can be formulated to a wide range of properties, they are generally of good strength and toughness, fairly flexible, and weather- and water-resistant.

Epoxy has exceptional adhesive strength and will bond with almost any material. Epoxies are sometimes reinforced with fiberglass to produce superior, if more costly, sheet material. Mixed with aggregate they are used to repair broken or spalled concrete and to resurface concrete floors. The mixture can even be drawn to the finest feather edge. By using marble chips as aggregate, a terrazzo finish of high durability can be formed, which is safe from chemical attack and waterproof. Finishing is similar to concrete terrazzo.

Caulking

Traditional caulking was a pasty mixture of pulverized limestone (calcium carbonate) and linseed oil. Eventually this cured to a hard substance and cracked and weathered away. Glazing compound, for the setting of glass, substituted mineral oil (a petroleum product), which is not a drying oil. This compound remained soft for a longer period. Both products are now generally replaced with various organic (or semi-organic) compounds with superior qualities of adhesion and endurance.

Adhesives were not very reliable before the development of synthetic organic compounds. Hide glue was neither very water-resistant nor long-lasting. Today it is difficult to imagine a world without the powerful adhesives now available.

There are many caulking and sealing compounds available. Most are equally suitable for glazing purposes. Some are two-part catalytic mixes; some are water-born polymers; others cure by solvent release. Some are formulated to solve certain problems, under the advice of experts. The following are the types most commonly in use at this time; however, new products arrive on the market at frequent intervals.

Acrylic latex is suitable for indoor or protected outdoor exposure. It adheres well to all materials, even when damp, except metal. An inexpensive water-base polymer, cleanup can be done simply with water. Although usually white, it is available in colors. The cured compound takes well to paint. Fresh latex caulk can be painted immediately with latex paint.

Butyl rubber is suitable for any exposure and adheres well to any dry material. A fairly inexpensive synthetic rubber, cleanup requires solvent. The color of butyl rubber is normally dark gray, but it can be painted when well cured.

Silicone is the most elastic, longest lasting product for caulking and adhesives. It is called semiorganic because the carbon radical is replaced with the equally amorphous element silica. Silicone adheres very well to every clean surface, although porous materials may need priming with a special product. Rather expensive, silicone is available in a limited variety of colors, which is sometimes a problem since paint will not adhere to the material.

Adhesives

Two general types of adhesives must be considered: those that are suitable for use on the construction site and those that require special shop conditions. Field use demands an adhesive with a relatively slow setting time, good filling capacity, ease of application, and the capacity to set over a wide temperature range without applied heat. Clamping is usually accomplished by nailing. In a shop, controlled conditions permit fast setting, machine application, high-pressure clamping, and heat for rapid curing. Many materials produced primarily for caulking, such as silicone, are also suitable as adhesives. Adhesives may be classified according to the process by which they set.

Solvent-release adhesives include all the water-born latexes such as the common white glue, polyvinyl acetate (PVA). These should not be used for nonporous surfaces, since the set depends upon penetration of the surfaces. They are very suitable for field use because they have good filling qualities and require no catalysts or heat to cure. PVA has good flexibility, permitting movement and expansion of the structure. Caution must be taken to avoid heavy exposure to moisture, since these adhesives are not highly water-resistant. Also included in this category are the mastic cements used for setting ceramic and resilient tile.

Polymerization is the chemical reaction that links molecules into long chains; it may be triggered by air contact, the addition of a catalyst, or heat. Polymers include phenolics, silicone, polyester, rubber, epoxy, and urethane. Those that rely upon air contact or catalysts are suitable for field use. They may be used with nonporous materials and are generally waterproof.

Thermoplastics are solids that liquify under heat and harden upon cooling. These include polyethylene, polymides, polyesters, and ethylene vinyl acetate (EVA). These are normally only used with shop equipment, where their quick setting time is advantageous. An exception is EVA, which is available in stick form for use with a portable melting tool.

Thermosetting adhesives include some polymers and rubbers, but also urea-formaldehyde resin, phenolic resin, the resorcinols, some epoxies, and melamine. Thermosetting plastics are liquids that harden with the application of heat and pressure; they are suitable only for shop work.

Contact cement is in a category of its own. Although it does require solvent release, this rubber adhesive never fully dries, retaining a permanent tacky stage. Contact cement is used by coating both surfaces to be joined, then allowing them to dry to the minimum tack. After careful positioning, the pieces are pressed together, joining them immediately and permanently. Contact cement is categorized as a pressure-sensitive adhesive and can be used in the field as well as at the shop. As it adheres well to porous and nonporous materials, it is especially well suited for the application of plastic laminate to a substrate.

Glass in Interiors

In the form of accessories and mirrors, glass is a part of almost every interior. Extensively used as a furniture component, glass is a popular material for table and desk tops, often as a protective surface for more delicate materials. However, with the development of tougher finishes, this use has become less common. While not generally a structural material, glass has been so used for some furniture, such as table supports and cube tables. More often glass is set in frames for doors of vitrines and cabinets. With the edges ground, glass may be used frameless as sliding doors for display cabinets. Such doors may be painted to become opaque and introduce color. Showcases in shops use glass extensively in the form of doors, fronts, and tops. In this manner exhibit cases are formed for museums.

Mirrors have been subject to fashion cycles. They have long been in use in frames for functional or decorative purposes; no bathroom can be without one. But twenty or thirty years ago mirrors were frequently used to create an illusion of larger space, often covering an entire wall. This is still common in commercial uses; in retail shops, mirrors can provide sparkle and illusion aside from the obvious requirements. In all likelihood they will return to the residence. Today, carefully detailed dressing rooms or bedrooms may have doors surfaced with mirrors for functional as well as decorative reasons.

Glass may be found as a component of interior partitions. Although "bank partitions" have declined in use since the emergence of systems furniture, there are still a good number of systems that offer glass as one of the possible infill materials. In many office buildings, glazed partitions are a necessity if natural light is desired for spaces remote from windows. Daylight may be "borrowed" from other spaces through the use of highly glazed areas in the inside partitions, while maintaining privacy. The various textures and tints available provide a wide range in optical clarity to meet the desired transparency.

Thick tempered glass is used to support handrails where maximum transparency is important. High cost is a factor limiting this use.

Considering its use for accessories and light fixtures, there can be little doubt that glass runs a close second to wood in popularity as an interior material.

Plastics in Interiors

Given the fact that plastics have been widely available only since the late 1940s, it may be surprising to discover how much they are now used in interiors. High-pressure laminates must lead the field by any measure of quantity. Hardly any interior space can be found that does not include some surface of plastic laminate. The photographic process makes identification difficult without close scrutiny. While they are fairly costly for wall surfaces, their durability and ease of maintenance make them practical for heavy traffic areas requiring ease of cleaning: medical facilities, kitchens, and restaurants. Plastic laminates are also the mainstay for countertops and cabinets in stores, eating places, public spaces, and the home kitchen, as well as for office desks and other furnishings.

Plastics have given rise to a whole new approach to furniture design. The new manufacturing processes represent a greater revolution in the industry than any past invention, including bentwood. The formation of shells for seating combines the seat, back, and even the arms into one unit in a single manufacturing operation. The shell chair was pioneered by Charles Eames and was designed to be used with or without a covering pad or fabric. Hundreds of similar chairs have since been designed, or copied. Reinforced with fiberglass, these plastic chairs are capable of withstanding heavy use.

Eero Saarinen developed a very elegant line of furniture using plastics for his "Pedestal Group," produced by Knoll International. However, not very many other leading furniture designers in the United States have used plastic, hence most of the products on the market are at the low end of the market and of not very good design. Italian designers have been interested in plastics for many years and have developed fine pieces, some of which have become classics.

Certain elements of furniture, such as drawers, can be molded in one piece, with obvious cost benefits compared with the construction of wood drawers. While chair shells are hot-pressed, smaller elements can be injection-molded. Other pieces are assembled from extruded parts, or a combination of the above. Plastics in general are water-resistant, making these products suitable for exterior use. Even iron furniture may be plasticized by dipping in liquid vinyl, which creates a lasting finish for indoors or out. An entire industry has grown around the production of plastic accessories such as storage bins, small shelves, and extensive lines of office and household products.

Resilient flooring and wallcoverings are an important use of plastic discussed elsewhere. Many fabrics are woven from or coated with plastic. Plastic coating may be applied to the surface of a fabric to create a synthetic leather, or to the back to provide greater durability. There is no doubt that the development of plastics has provided designers and manufacturers with new opportunities. Frequently manufacturers have not recognized the inherent qualities of the material and have used plastic to imitate any number of other materials: brick, stone, ceramic tile, and wood, of any texture or color.

Essentially inexpensive, plastic was often used for cheaply made objects. This has given the material an often undeserved reputation. The very term "plastic culture" implies a negative connotation referring to many aspects of contemporary life and culture aside from plastic itself. When used in a straightforward and honest way, plastic is one of the most useful and flexible materials at the disposal of designers.

11 Paint

Paint is a mixture of pigments with a hardening liquid or volatile thinner that will form a solid adherent film when applied to a surface for decoration or protection.

The earliest form of paint was the simple mixture of pigments, finely ground in water, applied to wet plaster—a process known as fresco, from the Italian *affresco*. Binding these pigments with egg white created a paint that would adhere to dry surfaces. This is called distemper or tempera. Modern oil paint was developed by the Flemish in the fifteenth century; the drying properties of linseed oil were used to produce a tough, lasting film. This oil was plentiful as a by-product of their flourishing linen industry. With this development, paints could be spread on any dry surface—indoors, outdoors, or on portable boards.

Lacquers, which are Oriental in origin, are made from various tree resins derived from fossil and living sources. These resins are dissolved in solvents that evaporate rapidly, allowing for quick recoating. Today most lacquers are synthetic nitrocellulose products. Modern paints are available compounded from a whole host of synthesized oils, latexes, resins, and other products. These provide a variety of somewhat bewildering choices for the designer. They are all proprietary compounds and the ingredients can be discussed only in the most general terms. No two manufacturers' products are quite the same, and a great deal of reliance must be placed upon the instructions of the manufacturer.

Trade Sales Paints

Products sold to the general public through retail outlets are called in the industry "trade sales" paints. The manufacturer must be aware that many of the users will be inexperienced in painting practice. Therefore the products must match displayed color cards and be safe and easy to use according to clear instructions on the container.

Paints of all types are composed of four basic ingredients: body, pigment, binder, and thinner. The latter two combined are referred to as the vehicle. Any number of additives—driers, fungicides, fillers, and others—may also be included.

The body provides the bulk of the film and the opacity for good coverage. The body materials are normally metallic salts. In years past, white lead (basic lead carbonate) was most commonly used. Since lead has been found to cause brain damage when ingested, most states have legislated against its use. Indeed, some states require the paint removal or resheathing of rental units with lead-based paint coatings. Zinc oxide is now used generally in lower quality paint; it is safe, but less opaque than lead. Because of its superior covering capability, at higher cost, titanium dioxide is usually the body ingredient in higher quality paints. All of these become white paint when used without additional pigment.

The pigment is the coloring ingredient. Many pigments are obtained from natural mineral sources, such as umber and sienna. Metallic salts, including chromium, iron, and copper, are common. More recently, many organic compounds have been synthesized, such as phthalo-cyanine and the anilines, providing a limitless color palette. In general, the minerals have better color retention (colorfastness) than the synthetics; but many organic pigments are quite resistant to fading and they all must be judged by their individual qualities.

All paint types use similar pigments and body compounds; the difference lies in the binders and their thinners. Most paints are available with gloss (shiny) or flat (dull) finish, and often with several degrees between. These are named variously: semigloss, satin, eggshell, and so forth. The degree of gloss depends upon the proportion of body to binder and is not very standardized. It should be noted that all paints go on glossy, the degree of flatness appearing as the paint cures.

The binders change from liquid to solid and unify the film, as well as adhering to the base. Together with the body compound they comprise most of the final skin of the coating and determine much of the paint quality and durability.

The thinners are added to help the paint flow more smoothly and to control the film thickness. They evaporate quickly, in a matter of hours or sometimes even minutes. The vehicle hardens more slowly, requiring many hours or even days, according to type.

Special paints are formulated for use as a first coat; these are known as primers. The desired quality for a primer is a high level of penetration and adherence to the surface. Durability is not to be expected, and the primer must soon be followed by one or more finish coats. To assure complete coverage with finish coats, each coat is sometimes tinted slightly differently.

Oil Paints. Oil paints use as a binder a drying, or curing, oil. This oil goes through the process of oxidation, which changes the liquid oil to a leathery film. Traditionally linseed oil is used, but fish, tung, castor, and other oils are also used for various reasons. The thinner of oil paint was traditionally turpentine, distilled from pine resin. Today it is much more likely to be mineral spirits, produced from petroleum. Oxidizers, called driers, are usually added to speed the curing process. In the face of declining supplies of natural drying oils, a synthetic, alkyd resin, was developed. It is now the leading oil for construction paints, leaving linseed oil mostly for special finishes and artists. Alkyd resin need not be viewed as an inferior substitute, however; for construction purposes, it has a level of quality often equal or superior to natural oil.

Oil paints are tough, reliable, and long-lasting. They are also messy, smelly, and intolerant of moisture. Not only can they not be painted on surfaces that are the least bit damp, but they fail to stick to surfaces if dampness comes from behind. It seems inevitable that latex paints should have been invented.

Latex Paints. Latex, the source of rubber, is now usually seen as a synthetic. While some latex is dissolved in solvent, principally for industrial use, the great bulk of latex is used as a water emulsion; that is, processed so that water may be the thinner. After the water evaporates, a chemical process called polymerization begins. By this process the small latex molecules begin to join together into longer chains. When complete, the film is no longer water-miscible. This is a slow process; latex films take about a month to become washable.

The two principal latex binders are vinyl chloride and acrylic resins. Paints with these binders are the most widely used for both interior and exterior applications today, with acrylic taking a commanding lead over vinyl for its superior qualities. These include greater durability and greater resistance to "bleeding" (the penetration of underlying stains). Both paints can be applied to a damp surface and will permit water vapor to escape through their porous film. Not the least reason for their popularity is their ease of cleanup, with water, and minimal odors.

Varnish. Varnish is essentially a nearly clear paint with transparent resins substituting for the metallic salt as the body. These resins were originally natural, tapped from living trees, such as dammar, or mined from deposits of fossil resins, such as copal. These natural resins are still in use by artists, but the commercial field has largely been taken over by synthetics. The construction industry is presently dominated by one such resin: polyurethane. "Urethane" varnishes actually represent a modification of alkyd resin, and the term "uralkyd" has been suggested as more descriptive, although this term has never caught on. This product is notably superior to natural resins in most measures of durability. The ideal "spar" varnish, suitable for natural exterior wood finish, still eludes us, however, due to the chemical breakdown of all organic compounds under exposure to ultraviolet radiation. Other synthetics used in varnish include the alkyd resins and tung phenolics. Others can be expected to appear from time to time in this rapidly expanding area.

Varnishes are available as gloss or dull ("satin") finish. The latter is accomplished by the addition of silicates, which diffuse reflections. Other common additives are driers and ultraviolet absorbers, which are added in an effort to reduce the effects of radiation. Experimental work continues to attempt to improve ultraviolet-resistance.

Enamel. Enamel paint is not to be confused with porcelain enamel, a melted-glass product requiring a high-temperature industrial process. Enamel paint is essentially pigmented varnish that is low in body material. Chief characteristics include high gloss and semitransparency. Some industrial enamels are rapidly cured by heating; they are known as "baked" enamels. Sometimes this rather inexact term is used to describe any highly glossy paint.

Lacquer. Lacquer, unlike varnish, contains no drying oils as binders. It is composed of practically clear resins dissolved in a thinner. Since various resins dissolve to a greater or lesser extent in different solvents, lacquer thinner is a complex mixture of esters, ethers, alcohols, and acetone. Lacquer is completely "cured" as soon as these highly volatile substances evaporate. This permits rapid and frequent recoating to create a deep and rich finish. The line between lacquer and varnish is a thin one. Varnish with a good deal of drying oil in the vehicle is called "long oil" varnish. When only a relatively small amount of drying oil is included, the product is "short oil" varnish. Here the relationship with lacquer becomes close indeed.

Shellac, a natural resin exuded by the Asian lac bug when feeding on the bark of certain trees, must be considered the original lacquer. Dissolved in alcohol, it produces a deep glowing finish formerly much prized for floors and pianos. Naturally of deep orange color, it is sometimes bleached to nearly white. It has poor resistance to water, however, and has largely fallen out of use as a wood finish. Today shellac is mainly used for its very high resistance to penetration by wood resins and marker and ballpoint inks; it is an excellent primer for these conditions. It is now available as a quick-drying primer with excellent adhesion. For this use, white body material is added to improve covering ability.

Modern lacquer, except for certain traditional Oriental products, is almost exclusively made with nitrocellulose. This is a highly explosive material, not for amateur use. Pigment is frequently added, but very little body material, so a semitransparent film is maintained. Many coats of lacquer may be applied in rapid succession; when rubbed with a fine abrasive compound between coats, lacquer produces a finish unparalleled in depth and luster.

Stains. Stains are essentially thin-bodied paints that leave little surface skin and are principally used to color wood. They may be of oil or latex base, which offer little protection to the wood, or of special vehicles designed to offer more protection. These latter include refined creosote and penetrating sealers. Creosote, a petroleum or coal-tar derivative, is toxic to insects and fungi. It is also highly aromatic. Because its long-term ecological effects are uncertain, its use is now discouraged.

Sealers penetrate the wood surface and coat the inner surfaces of the pores, offering water-resistance without building up surface skin. They sometimes are combined with toxic preservatives to double their effectiveness.

Exterior stains are usually pigmented with mineral salts for color-fastness. Those designed for interior use may use aniline dyes and leave no surface deposit at all; they are appropriate when weather-resistance is not a factor.

Industrial Finishes

All the above "trade sale" paints are formulated to give little trouble if the manufacturer's directions are followed. There are many industrial process paints not normally used on the construction site that have occasional applications, such as the epoxies.

Epoxy resin is a very tough water-resistant synthetic suitable for swimming pools, shower stalls, and other wet locations. It is most often supplied in the form of a two-package or catalytic curing system. The two parts are mixed just before use and have a limited working time. Epoxy is also made available in a solvent base for convenience. The evaporative fumes are very noxious, however, and epoxy should not be used in a confined space.

There are many other industrial finishes that have excellent special qualities, but which require highly controlled conditions or high curing temperatures. Among these are baked enamels, phenolic resins, and powdered coatings. However, these seldom have applications at the building site.

Application

Painting new material seldom poses many problems; the designer selects the proper primer and one or two finish coats as the manufacturer may recommend. When oil paint is used, surface dryness is of special concern, while latex emulsion requires the careful removal of any uncured oil.

Repainting old surfaces requires much more careful consideration. Thorough washing with a strong detergent such as TSP is necessary. Glossy finishes should be sanded to create "tooth" for the new coating. Severely deteriorated paint should be removed by chemical or heat stripping, or by mechanical scraping. New paint will endure only as well as the surface beneath. Painting over old wallpaper or vinyl covering can seldom yield satisfactory results. The skin tension created by the curing process may curl the edges and bubble the surface. Removal of such materials is always best.

Paint in very poor condition may be a warning of problems beyond the surface coating. Peeling or bubbling paint may indicate wetting from behind, which must be corrected first. Beware of deteriorated plaster; in old buildings only the paint skin may be holding it in place. Such a surface can only be replaced or covered with new material.

Paint in Interiors

Paint covers more interior surfaces than any other finish material. Not only are walls and ceilings painted more often than not, so is a great deal of furniture, woodwork, floors, paneling, and anything else that might be used in an interior. Paint is also the least expensive design element for interiors. This factor is often forgotten by those who regard paint as merely a necessary finish for walls and ceilings.

Paint usually means color, and an interior space can be totally transformed by different colors alone. Paint can create the mood and ambience in spaces, varying from dramatic and delightful to severe and dismal. Few interior spaces, except perhaps photographers' darkrooms, are painted black. Clearly such surfaces would reflect little light and make the space difficult to live with. The fact that white or light colors are in most prevalent use for interiors demonstrates the importance of reflectance and quality of light as a component of design.

Numerous studies have been done by behavioral scientists trying to determine the effect of color on human conduct. Despite many theories, no conclusive evidence has been obtained, and the theories have been refuted and changed continuously. Perhaps the residual fact is that while color does have an influence upon the way people act and feel, there seems to be no universal answer to the question *how*. Recent research in California found that rooms painted a strong pink color had a calming effect upon violent prisoners and mentally disturbed inmates; however, the effect was only temporary.

Paint, for interior designers, is an unequaled creative tool. Some designers, as well as the public, are inclined to work with whatever colors are the fashion of the moment. Frequently, fashion is determined by successful designers, but fashion is also made by the manufacturers of paint, of fabrics, and of floorcoverings. Through extensive advertising campaigns certain colors are made the "current" colors. This often results in meaningless and even poor color schemes. Some years ago it became fashionable for interiors to be painted green and complemented by a green carpeting. The results were tasteless, but there are many "period" pieces from the fifties era of trend-setting colors.

More recently, certain pastel shades have become fashionable, popularized through the work of the leading Postmodernist designers. More than anyone, the architect Michael Graves influenced this color trend in reaction to the decades when, under the influence of the International School, the most fashionable interior color was plain white.

The way paint colors can be used is limited only by the imagination of the designer. Entire rooms can be white or one color. But a room can also be painted all white except for one wall, which is painted in a strong accent color. So may color be used on moldings or other architectural components as a contrast to the dominant wall colors.

As mentioned at the beginning of the chapter, the earliest examples of painted decoration were frescoes. In subsequent eras, painting on walls and ceilings became the vehicle of expression for some of history's greatest artists. In the sixties, after years of white spaces and interiors with little color, it became fashionable to use graphics and super-graphics. Another traditional painted art form to regain popularity is the use of trompe l'oeil in interiors. This fooling of the eye is used to apparently change the size or shape of space.

Postmodernism in architecture and design has brought about some interesting painted decorations, as well as the typical colors associated with the movement. The term "ornamentalism" is perhaps a better way to describe this fashionable direction. This is apparent in architecture, in interior design, and in furniture design, as well as in the fine arts. In interiors, interest has revived in stenciling and other patterned decorations. Furniture is being decorated with paint in striking patterns and colors. The stenciling of floors, a form of decoration used in Colonial America, has reappeared.

The changing fashions and trends in interior design have brought about the return of glossy paints and enamels for elegant residences, thickly lacquered furniture in bright colors (now with excellent stain- and water-resistance), and elegant wood furniture stained with penetrating aniline dyes.

12 Wall, Flooring, and Ceiling Surface Materials

The material that makes up the structure for floors, walls, and ceilings may often be left as the final surface. But from prehistoric times, the desire to provide better protection from the elements, or to ornament the surfaces, or simply to provide an agreeable tactile environment has led to a proliferation of materials used solely as a surface finish. While some materials may be suitable for any floor, wall, or ceiling, other materials will predominate in one location or another.

Wall Surface Materials

Walls may be formed of the natural material composing the structure: stone, brick, glass, plastic laminate, wood, plaster, and/or drywall. These may or may not be painted or otherwise coated. Such surfacings are treated under the appropriate sections.

The earliest use of wallpaper was centuries back in the Orient. In Europe, wallpaper has been in use since the sixteenth century, in the United States since the early Colonial period. In the beginning, wallpaper was used as an inexpensive alternative to tapestries and wall fabrics, which had been used to reduce drafts and coldness of surfaces in stone halls. While little protection can be gained from wallpaper, the better building technology that emerged in the eighteenth century eliminated the need for cloth hangings. From the nineteenth century to today, wallpaper has been the most popular interior surfacing material (other than paint). Vinyl wallcoverings became available around the middle of the twentieth century. Durable and easily cleaned, they probably are the most innovative wall surfacing of the twentieth century.

Wallpaper. Papers manufactured for the mass market are printed by rollers in repeat patterns. The exception is "mural" designs, when several sheets are prepared to be joined to form a larger design. These patterns have been little used by modern designers, but for the rare occasion of period reproduction or for historic restoration. Even the most handsome patterns and designs that are available tend to be overwhelming when used on all walls, not to mention the ceiling as well. A few fine-quality papers may be so subtle and beautifully printed that they can be used to create a favorable environment. Generally, a more interesting effect may be obtained by singling out certain walls or areas for bold patterns as accents.

Some wallpaper is available with clear plastic coating. This process adds to the cost, but is very beneficial in terms of maintenance. Their life expectancy in such high-moisture areas as kitchens and bathrooms is more than double that of uncoated papers. These coated papers are more durable than uncoated papers, but not as strong as the vinyl coverings listed below.

Very elegant results may be obtained by the use of natural wallcoverings, textured rather than patterned. An example is Japanese grasscloth, which is made by tying together dried grass into long strands and cementing them close together to fine paper. The grass may be dyed and the paper colored to provide great color choice to the designer. Another option is fine linen laminated to paper backing; other cloth is also used, including delicate Shiki silk. Another popular natural material is cork that is sliced paper-thin and mounted to a paper backing. These textured wallcoverings have some acoustical absorption value and are used in nonresidential spaces as well as in the home. They will stand normal usage for many years and, if properly installed, may be painted, endowing them with a second life. Caution must be taken to use oil-based paint, as water-based paint may loosen the paste anchoring the paper and cause bubbling.

Wallpaper installation requires good knowledge of the necessary materials. Wallpaper is packaged as a standard roll 20½″ (52 cm) wide and 21′ (6.4 m) long. In practice, wallpaper is always sold as a double roll 42′ (12.8 m) long. Wallpaper is often expected to cover damaged or decayed plaster walls. This cannot be successful unless the walls are prepared properly. Such a wall must be filled, smoothed, and sanded, then sized with a glue solution. A liner of kraft paper should be applied before the final wallcovering. Paperhanger's paste must be applied to the backs of both the kraft paper and the wallpaper before they are put on the wall. This paste expands the paper so that it shrinks tightly when dry. A good professional wallpaper hanger will work in this fashion, which is most important when fine papers are used.

Vinyl Wallcoverings. These materials are available in all price ranges and gauges. For domestic use they are often similar to plastic-coated paper, but capable of providing much more service. Properly installed in bathrooms and other high-humidity areas, the vinyls will hold up long after any paper has begun to degenerate. The strongest and most serviceable wallcoverings are fabrics coated with vinyl (PVC). These are available in much greater widths, 54″ (1.37 m) being most common, and longer rolls than wallpaper. This is possible in part because they are not subject to expansion and contraction with moisture changes. The heaviest grades are manufactured for institutional use and, while expensive, may be expected to give many years of service. In public and institutional buildings these wallcoverings may provide significant savings because vinyl fabrics can be cleaned easily, while paint has to be applied frequently. The median rate for paint application in commercial spaces is three years, while the expected replacement rate for vinyl wallcovering is ten years. This is particularly important in spaces where cleanliness is paramount.

Vinyl wallcoverings are produced in three grades: light, medium, and heavy duty. Light-duty wallcovering is produced on a scrim backing with a weight between 7 and 13 ounces (200 and 340 g) per square yard (.914 m²). This type provides moderate protection in light-duty areas where a decorative surface is desired. It is the most common weight for residential application.

Medium-duty wallcovering is produced on Osnaburg or Drill backing and weighs between 13 and 22 ounces (340 and 620 g) per square yard (.914 m²). This weight is commonly used for all commercial and institutional applications.

Heavy-duty wallcovering is produced on a broken twill fabric backing and weighs in excess of 22 ounces (620 g) per square yard (.914 m²). This is used as a wallcovering for areas subject to extraordinarily heavy use, such as hospital corridors, elevator foyers, and food-service areas.

As a plastic material, vinyl is available in all possible colors and textures, often in imitation of natural materials including grasscloth, fabrics of all kinds, leathers, and even travertine. In the better grades, this imitation is all but indetectable from some of the real materials. Some original textures are also created especially for the material, such as the currently popular "suede." The deeper textures may have some acoustical absorption value. While the appearance of the heavier grades of vinyl-covered fabrics varies widely, quality has much improved over the years, perhaps because these materials are specified by designers, rather than sold directly to the consumer.

Fabrics. Widespread in the eighteenth and nineteenth centuries, fabric wallcoverings are very much in evidence today. They may range from the simple painter's canvas and burlap to the most costly silks. Canvas is sometimes used to cement together crumbling walls and ceilings; it does, however, have an interesting texture in its own right. Painter's canvas is sized and made to be painted, even when used as a wall-surfacing material. As mentioned, some fine fabrics are available already laminated to paper for installation like wallpaper.

While almost any fabric can be laminated to a backing to facilitate installation as a surfacing, as a custom process, lamination is costly. Besides lamination, there are two common methods for installing fabrics as wall surfacing. The first is to install wooden tack strips along the fabric's edges and seams, then stretch and tack the material into place. The space between the strips is often filled with fiber batts or foam rubber to cushion the surface and to enhance the acoustical qualities of the wall.

The second method is for use with heavier fabrics, which may be simply hung from the top, with no attempt to stretch them smooth; they may even be draped. When heavier fabrics are applied to surfaces, the finished appearance resembles upholstery, which may be exactly the effect desired. Felt makes one of the best acoustical wall surfaces and is available in many colors and several grades based on thickness. The heavier grades may be cemented directly to the base surface, like carpeting, which is discussed in another section.

Ceramics

Ceramics are products made from a nonmetallic mineral by firing at high temperatures, thus uniting the particles.

Terra-cotta, from the Italian for cooked earth, is a clay product fired at a relatively low temperature. It is used for statuary and architectural ornament and surfacing. Usually terra-cotta is of a nonmodular, nonstructural nature.

Quarry tile is an unglazed modular tile principally used for paving. It is extruded or dry-pressed of clay essentially of the type and colors used to produce brick.

Glazed ceramic tile is a thin modular tile of fine pottery clay that is fired at a high temperature, then refired for glazing. Usually used for wall surfacing, these tiles may be used for floor surfacing if a durable, nonslip glaze is used.

Vitreous tile is a thin unglazed tile. It is made of special clays fired to a very high temperature so that vitrification (glasslike fusion) occurs.

The difference between brick and other fired clay materials is somewhat artificial; brick is normally classified as a modular, structural material, and tiles are considered as materials serving as finished surfacing. The glazed brick surfacing of the gates of Babylon, at an excess of four thousand years of age, must rate as the earliest ceramic facing. It is clear that the prehistoric Greek and Etruscan temples were built of wood with terra-cotta facings, beginning a tradition of terra-cotta ornamental facing that reached mastery in modern times with the highly original work of Louis Sullivan and Frank Lloyd Wright. Early mosaic surfaces were of tiny bits (tesserae) of colored stone and glass assembled into a design and set in mortar. Commonly used as flooring by the Romans, mosaic reached its peak with the Byzantine Empire. Entire interior surfaces, walls, arches, and domes were covered with tesserae as small as ⅛″ (3 mm) square; these created elaborate works of art. Today mosaic tiles are usually considered ceramic pieces that are not less than 1″ (25 mm) square.

The first large-scale use of glazed ceramic tile appeared in Islamic architecture of the Middle Ages. Excellent surfaces from the fourteenth century also survive in the Alhambra. This tradition of glazed painted tiles spread throughout the Mediterranean basin and was called majolica, faience, or Faenza, accordingly made in Spain, France, or Italy, although the names are often interchanged. In the north, Delft, a city in Holland, became famous for its porcelain tiles with blue designs.

Architectural Terra-Cotta. More often than not, the term terra-cotta refers to large modular glazed ceramic panels used for exterior facing. There is a long tradition, however, for more creative works, termed architectural terra-cotta. Based upon the drawings of the designer, the full area to be covered is modeled in Plasticine. After approval, the model is divided into conveniently sized pieces with the insertion of projecting brass strips. Plaster of paris is then poured between the strips to create molds. The molds are hand-packed with ceramic clay material at a fairly uniform thickness of ½" to ¾" (13 to 19 mm). The edges are made thicker, and, if necessary for reinforcement, ribs may be made at intervals to the plane of the edge. Notches may also be provided in the edges for hangers. The Plasticine original is usually damaged by the process, but the plaster molds can be reused a number of times. After drying, the ceramic pieces may be coated with slip, for color, then redried and fired. The terra-cotta may be painted and coated with clear glaze, or color-glazed and refired.

Before the terra-cotta is shipped to the project site, its edges, warped by the firing, are ground for a close fit. The pieces are numbered and an installation diagram is prepared. Small pieces of terra-cotta may be set in mortar, but larger ones are supported with metal hangers. The joints are pointed with mortar or, more likely today, with elastic sealant.

Setting Tile. All modular tile is set in a similar manner. Traditionally the tiles are set in a mortar bed about ¾" (19 mm) thick. When walls are to be tiled, wire or expanded metal lath is first secured to the backing. Because the mortar is a rather dry mix, the tiles are soaked in water before installation. Upon application to the mortar, the wet tile adheres quickly as it loses some of its moisture to the cement. The joints may then be grouted (filled) with a fine cement-lime mixture. This method will allow the tile-setter to slope a floor to drain, if there are floor drains. For this reason mortar-bed setting is still frequently used for floors in commercial and institutional interiors.

Floor levels must be considered when changing materials. In new construction, floor areas to be tiled are recessed 1" (25 mm) or more when sloping some distance to drain. In existing construction, it may be necessary to elevate the floor areas that are to receive other finishes.

Today, tile is more likely to be set by the thin-set method. With this method, a solid backing of water-resistant gypsum board or plywood is installed. A thin coat of waterproof cement may next be applied, to protect the backing, and then a fresh layer of a specially formulated organic mastic cement is applied with a toothed trowel to increase the resilience of the cement. Dry tiles are then pressed into the cement. Grouting is done in the conventional manner. To speed the process, tiles are often mounted on an open-mesh cloth backing in 1′ (300 mm) squares, especially in the smaller sizes. Some even are pregrouted with an elastic compound. A great variety of shapes are produced for trim, including cushion edges, inside and outside corners, coves, and bases. Bullnose ends can compensate for the mortar bed, if required.

The thickness of glazed tiles is fairly standard at $5/16″$ (8 mm). By old standards they measured $4¼″$ (108 mm) square. They are available today, however, in a great number of sizes, ranging from as small as $3/8″$ (10 mm) square to 6″ (150 mm) square. Nor are they by any means restricted to square; many shapes—rectangles, hexagons, and even circles—are available to confound the designer.

TILE SPECIAL SHAPES

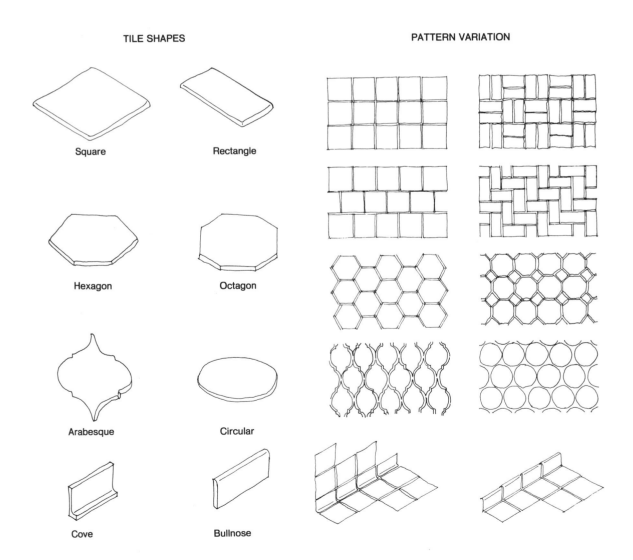

TILE SHAPES

Square

Rectangle

Hexagon

Octagon

Arabesque

Circular

Cove

Bullnose

PATTERN VARIATION

Quarry Tile. Unglazed, quarry tile, at ½" (13 mm), is generally thicker than glazed tile. They are also most often larger, 6" (150 mm) square, 6" × 12" (150 mm × 300 mm), to 12" (300 mm) square. Fabricated from the same kind of clay as brick, they often are made in the size of brick pavers to simulate brick without the more difficult thickness. For a more water- and soil-resistant floor, quarry tiles may be salt-glazed in the first firing; these are called "pavers." Quarry tile is usually set in mortar, but over the appropriate surface the tiles may be thin-set in the manner of glazed tile. For terraces over inside spaces, a layer of sand may be spread over a waterproof membrane before the mortar and quarry tile is applied. However the tile is installed, the joints are ⅜" (10 mm) wide and grouting is done with normal brick mortar.

Vitreous Tile. Sometimes called ceramic mosaic tile, vitreous tile is fired at high temperature to become a glasslike material. Its gritty unglazed surface makes a nonslip surface suitable for flooring. Despite their thinness (¼" or 6 mm), these tiles also wear well; they are very hard and the same color throughout. They are small, generally 1" × 1", 1" × 2", or 2" × 2" (25 × 25, 25 × 50, or 50 × 50 mm). They are by no means restricted to rectangular shapes; hexagons, octagons, and combined sizes are popular. The lack of glaze does not restrict color choice. Mineral pigments added to the clay give a great variety of hues and shades.

Flooring

Many of the ceramics mentioned above are used for flooring. Concrete (including terrazzo), bricks, plastics, wood, and carpets are considered in the appropriate sections. Here only those materials used almost exclusively for flooring are discussed.

Resilient Flooring. Resilient flooring may be any of a number of flooring materials in tile or sheet form of more or less resilient body. Although the ancient Egyptians apparently used native asphalt as a flooring as well as a roofing material, resilient flooring as it is considered today is a recent innovation in building. Linoleum, the first, originated in the nineteenth century; it is composed of natural materials. Asphaltic compounds were the first resilient flooring materials to be formed as tiles and became very widespread in use in the early twentieth century. The plastics industry, stimulated by the shortages of some natural materials brought about by the restriction of imports during World War II, soon captured the resilient flooring industry, with vinyl in some form as the distant leader.

Linoleum. Basically a mixture of ground cork and linseed oil, linoleum may also include wood flour and other additives in proprietary admixtures. This mixture is spread to uniform thickness over burlap backing, and the oil curing is hastened by controlled heat. Produced in widths as great as 9′ (2.74 m), linoleum sheets are easily trimmed to fit irregular spaces and are cemented to a suitable subfloor with linoleum paste. Where unavoidable, the joints are simply to be endured. Normally linoleum is produced in two thicknesses: .05″ and ⅛″ (1.27 and 3 mm). The heavier gauge is often called "battleship" linoleum, less because it might have been used on warships than for its presumed invulnerability. In truth, linoleum does make a very durable wearing surface; it is often found in good condition after many decades of use.

Pigments to produce any color can be introduced. Various colors can be die cut and fitted together in many patterns, which are then cemented to a secondary backing to produce "inlaid" linoleum. Patterns can be laid down during installation; borders of contrasting colors were popular during the 1920s and 1930s.

The above paragraphs might be written in the past tense, since linoleum flooring is hardly produced in the United States any longer. There still exists a small market for those who use linoleum as an easy surface to cut for block printing. The disappearance of linoleum as flooring is less a qualitative problem than an economic one. The newer plastics are cheaper both in materials and process. However, linoleum will still be found, often serving well, in many older buildings.

Asphalt Tile. While asphalt is found in the native state, from evaporated pools of petroleum, most asphalt today is the residue left after the more volatile products are distilled from crude oil. This is mixed with asbestos and powdered limestone, then consolidated under pressure to form sheets of the same thickness as linoleum. The sheets are cut into squares of either 9″ or 12″ (230 mm or 300 mm). Pigments can be added, but can produce only dark tones. The prime virtue of asphalt tiles is low cost, though they are quite wear-resistant.

Once again this product might be mentioned in the past tense, since it, too, has disappeared from the market. This time it is not economic factors, but quality that is at fault. Asphalt tiles are hard and brittle and do not recover well from impressions caused by long-standing furniture. While water-resistant, they also suffer damage from many solvents and oils. In addition, few designers were happy with the somber color range. Asphalt tile may still be found in older buildings, but seldom in good condition.

Rubber Flooring. Rubber flooring, now synthetic, was the first to rival asphalt tile for higher budget projects. Durable, with good dent-resistance, rubber can suffer damage from petroleum solvents and oils. Rubber seemed to be in the process of being driven from the market by vinyl until flooring created by the famous Italian automobile tire manufacturer Pirelli in the 1960s brought about a revival.

Cork Tile. In the manufacture of cork tile, chips of cork, mixed with resin binders, are rolled into sheets of various thicknesses; ⅛″, ³⁄₁₆″, and ¼″ (3, 4.8, and 6 mm) are the most common. Tile sizes range from 6″ × 6″ to 12″ × 24″ (150 × 150 to 300 × 600 mm). The surface is prefinished with wax or a clear vinyl coating. The varying degrees of darkness of the cork and the resin produce many shades of warm natural tones.

Cork tile is warm to the touch, quiet underfoot, and truly resilient. It is, however, only fair in durability and resistance to water and oil. All of the flooring called vinyl is composed, at least in part, of polyvinyl chloride (PVC). The two basic types are vinyl-asbestos and solid (or "pure") vinyl, with a good many variations. They are all of good durability: water-, oil-, and solvent-resistant. Beyond these qualities, there are notable differences.

Vinyl-asbestos is, as the name signifies, vinyl mixed with asbestos and other fillers. This material is less expensive than pure vinyl, but is also more brittle and less dent-resistant. The brittleness makes vinyl-asbestos suitable only for tile, in 9″ and 12″ (230 and 300 mm) squares. These tiles are generally available in .080″ and ⅛″ (2 and 3 mm) thicknesses. With light-colored basic ingredients, a wide range of colors is possible with vinyl-asbestos, while its considerable resilience allows textures to be impressed: brick, flagstone, and travertine, for example. Usually marbleized, vinyl-asbestos tile is also available in solid colors, at higher cost, however, because of the control required during manufacture. Recently the use of vinyl-asbestos has been called into question because of the asbestos content.

Vinyl flooring is more or less pure PVC. It is tough and flexible, which permits it to be produced in large sheets as well as tiles. It has all the possibilities inherent to vinyl-asbestos and, in addition, is more durable, dent-resistant, and easy to maintain. Pure vinyl can be produced in any degree of translucence; this imparts a certain depth of surface as well as realistic marble tones. Opaque bits of vinyl may be embedded in clear vinyl to resemble the tesserae of mosaics. Thinner sheets of vinyl can be cemented to foam backing to produce a truly resilient flooring. Sheet vinyl comes in widths of up to 9′ (2.74 m) and great lengths. A skilled installer can leave joints that are virtually invisible. Some sheet vinyls can be heat-welded by a highly skilled installer to leave no visible joints at all.

A full line of accessories to flooring are available in vinyl: molded bases, stair treads, thresholds, and tapered edge strips to minimize level changes. These are often used even with flooring other than vinyl.

Installation. No resilient flooring can be better than the base upon which it is cemented. Any irregularities will read through in time. With new construction, most often a smooth underlayment of particle board is cemented to the subfloor and the joints then filled. A good cement-finish concrete slab is satisfactory alone.

When reflooring, great care must be taken to prepare the old work. All surfaces must be clean and free from oil or wax. Old concrete must be repaired, smoothed, and filled with mastic underlayment cement. Wood or old resilient floors may be repaired the same way or covered with underlayment board if the thickness can be permitted.

The new flooring must be cemented down with the proper adhesive recommended for the material. Rolling the flooring with an 80# (36 kg) or more roller will force out air bubbles and eliminate minor irregularities. This is work for a skilled professional, and the manufacturer's instructions must be followed.

Monolithic Flooring. Cement-finished concrete and terrazzo are examples of flooring that is created on the site. There are also some resilient materials that are in this category, beginning with the ancient use of asphalt. The greatest advantage to these systems is their seamlessness and ability to level and fill uneven or damaged surfaces. They harden by the evaporation of solvents or water emulsions, or through chemical action including catalytic reaction.

Asphalt mastic flooring may be one of any number of possible combinations of asphalt, portland cement, and aggregate. This is then screeded over a suitable base and troweled to a compact finish. Such a flooring will be water-resistant and easily repairable. It will not, however, be highly durable or resistant to solvents and oils.

Magnesite is a compound of magnesium oxychloride cement mixed with fibers and pigments. It can be spread over any firm subfloor, usually in two layers. The first layer is heavily fibered for reinforcement; the second, thinner layer is pigmented. Such a floor is resilient and fire-resistant. The fact that it is not highly water-resistant or especially durable has caused magnesite largely to give way to the new organic plastics. It may still serve as a filler for old floors or in remodeling work.

Plastic flooring may be one of a number of organic resins that can be used for monolithic flooring over any sound base. These include epoxy, polyester, acrylic, and polyurethane, with various additives: fillers, pigments, colored plastic chips. These may be sprayed, poured, or troweled to a thickness ranging from ⅛″ to ½″ (3 to 12 mm). They are all proprietary products with varying qualities; they should be installed by licensed contractors. The epoxies are generally superior to the other resins or latexes, but all may be expected to be durable, chemical-resistant, and flexible.

Ceilings

Ceilings may well be the exposed wood, steel, or concrete structure. Plaster or drywall process may be applied and painted or otherwise coated. These are treated in the appropriate sections.

Almost any material used for wallcoverings, or for that matter floorcoverings, can be used as a finish ceiling. The materials that serve almost exclusively for ceilings are listed here. The purpose of installing a ceiling may go far beyond the desire to cover rough construction; the ceiling may become the major element for acoustical control of the space. It may allow space for mechanical-equipment requirements and provide outlets for heating, ventilating, and air conditioning. In addition, the ceiling may house recessed or indirect light fixtures.

Suspended Ceilings. The section on plaster and drywall describes suspended ceiling systems for that purpose. Other systems are available to support prepared panels or tiles.

The most common system in use is the T-bar suspension system, which is in the form of suspended enameled upside-down T-shaped metal bars. The grid may be suspended directly from open-web joists or, if necessary, from ¾" (19 mm) cold-rolled-steel channels. The channels are suspended, in turn, by wires secured to the structure above. If longer spans are necessary, the channels may be wired to larger channels. The most common grid size is 2' × 4' (60 × 120 cm); panels of various materials are simply dropped in. Fluorescent fixtures are designed to fit this module, as they are also designed to fit a 2' × 2' (60 × 60 cm) grid, the next most popular size. The 2' (60 cm) dimension is seldom varied because of the span limitation of the panel.

The panels usually have some sound-absorbing value and are most commonly composed of mineral or glass fibers. These fibers are mixed with a binder and molded; the surface is then coated with paint or plastic sheet. Any surface texture desired can be impressed. The texture may enhance the acoustical value of the panel, or may be only for decoration. The most popular acoustical patterns are regular rows of holes, random patterns of holes of different sizes, and fissures. In some systems the panel edge is rebated, recessing the suspension grid. The grid may be painted to match or contrast with the panels. In every case the dominant pattern is the grid.

If acoustical absorption is not desired, as may be the case in halls for speaking or music, panels of harder surface may be preferred. These can be finished with painted asbestos-cement or even mirror-finish aluminum.

The strong pattern created by the exposed T-bar suspension system is not always desired by the designer. To eliminate this enforced pattern, the Z-spline suspension system was devised. This specially formed metal spline is clipped to the channel irons and inserted into a kerf in the edge of the tiles. The upper part of the tile is relieved (cut back) to accommodate the spline. By this means, the edges of the tiles, which range in size from 6" × 12" (150 × 300 mm) to 9" and 12" (230 and 300 mm) square, are butted closely together. The edges may be beveled, to conceal slight variations and to articulate the individual tiles, or they may be square-edged. With sufficient precision on the part of the

SUSPENDED ACOUSTIC PANEL SYSTEMS

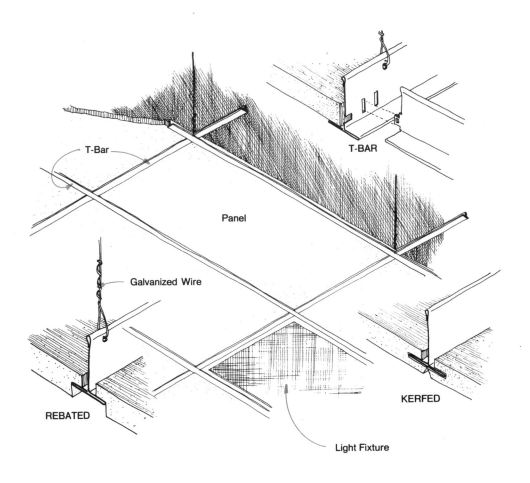

T-Bar

T-BAR

Panel

Galvanized Wire

REBATED

KERFED

Light Fixture

ALUMINUM CEILING

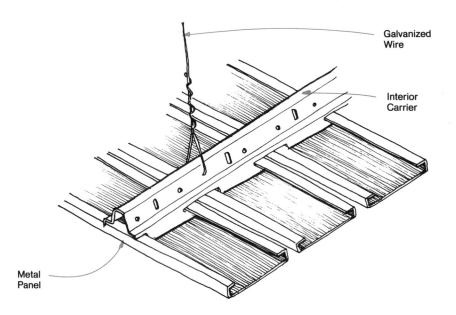

Galvanized
Wire

Interior
Carrier

Metal
Panel

installer, the latter type may be installed with almost indiscernible joints. All the same materials and patterns produced for the exposed grid system are available for the Z-spline. A patent system can permit these tiles to be pulled down and replaced, for access to space above.

This system can be installed to provide as high as a two-hour fire protection to the structure above. Of course, no openings for light fixtures or any other purpose can be permitted.

When the need for acoustical treatment to an existing flat ceiling is perceived, tiles can be cemented directly to the ceiling. They have similar characteristics to the tiles used for the Z-spline system and are secured with a mastic cement recommended by the manufacturer. In some cases, wood furring strips are applied to the structure above. Tongue-and-grooved tiles can be secured to these strips by concealed staples.

Aluminum ceilings are another option. Long, channel shaped aluminum strips are clipped to suspended support systems. They are spaced apart by a fraction of an inch and have fiberglass batts laid above to give sound-absorbing qualities to the system. The aluminum may be painted or polished and chromed to a mirror finish.

Most of the purposes of a ceiling can be accomplished by a suspended grid or a row of baffles. These may be of wood or any number of other materials. If the ceiling space is painted a dark tone and all lighting is directed downward from the level of the grid or baffle, an illusion of a ceiling is formed. In fact, if care is exercised, the baffle or grid can be eliminated and the illusion of a ceiling can be created by lights and paint alone.

At the risk of belaboring the obvious, it should be clear that the surfaces discussed constitute the form and limits to all interiors. The first and foremost consideration must be given to their selection.

13 Fabrics

Fabric is a pliable material made by weaving, felting, or knitting natural or synthetic fibers or filaments.

Fibers are pliable threadlike strands that can be spun into yarn. Over a thousand different fibers are available, but only about forty are of commercial importance.

The earliest evidence of woven cloth dates back to about 5000 B.C. These very early basketry weaves show that textiles of most natural fibers were already in use in ancient Egypt. By 3000 B.C., cotton was in use in India. Many other civilizations left examples of weaving that were often strikingly beautiful. By the fourth century B.C., India and China had developed a fairly sophisticated craft of weaving. Evidence has made clear that the Romans had dyed fabrics by the second century B.C. From ancient times, Persian textiles have been found, including carpets and tapestries. By the Middle Ages, Turkish tribes were known to have manufactured carpets and felts.

Textile industries eventually developed in Europe; by 1500, silk, linen, and wool were woven in all countries. While weaving was practiced in America long before the arrival of European settlers, the first textile mill of European pattern was established during the seventeenth century in Massachusetts. Until the onset of the Industrial Revolution, textile weaving remained essentially a cottage industry. The invention of the flying shuttle in 1733 led to the rapid growth of the industry, especially in England. The development of power looms heralded increasing automation during the nineteenth century, leading to the highly automated mills of today.

Synthetic fibers were searched for as early as the seventeenth century in an effort to find a substitute for silk. Experimental development began in Europe in the nineteenth century. The first commercial production of a new fiber, named rayon, began in the United States in 1910. This was followed by acetate in 1924 and glass fibers in 1936. The production of nylon by du Pont in 1939 made the greatest commercial impact, but the popular new material was soon diverted exclusively to the war effort. More and more synthetics were developed after the end of World War II. Now about 70 percent of all fibers used in the United States are synthetic—a clear indication of a trend that will continue into the future.

Natural Fibers

Natural fibers are of cellulose, such as cotton and linen, or of protein, such as wool and silk. The sole natural mineral fiber, asbestos, is not used in fabric for interior design.

Cotton is the most widely used natural fiber. That it is relatively durable and inexpensive accounts for its dominance of the textile market until the emergence of synthetics. The tensile strength of natural cotton may be enhanced by a process called mercerization, a chemical treatment with sodium hydroxide that increases the luster of the fiber as well as its strength.

Linen is the name for the cloth made from the bast fibers of the flax plant. Long popular for its strength and durability, linen is now viewed as a rather luxurious commodity. Higher quality fabrics are made from long-staple fibers, but most linens used for interiors are of short-staple fibers called tow. These linens are popular for draperies and wallcoverings. Their tendency to wrinkle can be reduced by treatment with a special wrinkle-resisting finish. Other bast fibers of commercial importance are sisal, jute, and hemp.

Silk has long been considered the most elegant of fibers. Made of the protein filament from the cocoon of the silk worm by a very costly process, silk has a high price that makes it less widely used today than in the past. While it has many desirable qualities and great luxury, silk requires a good deal of care. It does not stand up well to direct sunlight and does not have the strength required for many interior applications.

Wool is the dominant protein fiber, derived from the fleece of domesticated sheep that have been bred for thousands of years for that specific purpose. Although wool is relatively expensive, it continues to be very popular with designers for interior use. Depending upon the weave, wool can be made into very strong fabrics. Blended with other fibers, wool may develop various qualities, including economy. The strength and weight of the fibers make wool fabrics particularly suitable for heavy-duty upholstery. Pure wool fabrics are considered prestigious and elegant materials; they are indeed among the most beautiful fabrics. Whether woven into a smooth or rough-textured weave, they are both handsome and pleasant to the touch. They can be easily handled for any shape of upholstery or other application.

Speciality hair fibers such as mohair, camel's hair, and cashmere are not as widely available as wool and are not of major significance in the industry. These fabrics are used more for garments than for interior applications.

Synthetics. Synthetic fibers are filaments made by forcing a plastic substance through a miniscule nozzle called a spinnerette. The generic categories of fibers in the cellulosic family are acetate, rayon, and triacetate. In the noncellulosic family they are acrylic, aramid, glass, metallic fibers, modacrylic, nylon, olefin, polyester, saran, Spandex, and vinyon. Anidex, azlon, novolid, nytril, and vinal are not currently being produced in the United States.

Acetate has a luxurious appearance and drapes well. It is fairly soil-resistant and somewhat flame-retardant, also shrink- and moth-resistant. With all these qualities acetate is rather economical. On the negative side, it does not stand up well to sunlight and has low abrasion-resistance.

Rayon is soft and comfortable, highly absorbent, and easy to dye. Relatively inexpensive, it is a very versatile fiber. Rayon also has poor light-resistance and only variable abrasion-resistance, with low stability and resilience.

Triacetate is similar in most respects to acetate. It is used primarily for garments, and only rarely for fabrics in the furnishings industry.

Acrylics are soft and similar to wool in appearance. They are light-resistant and dimensionally stable; they are also slow to soil. They are not flame-resistant, however, and they have poor resistance to static electricity unless they are properly treated.

Glass makes a low-cost light-resistant and fireproof fiber that is dimensionally stable and quick-drying. Glass fibers do, however, have poor abrasion-resistance, cannot be dyed after fabrication, and have an unpleasant feel.

Metallic fibers are used as components of blended fiber fabrics and do not represent a significant volume of material in the furnishings industry.

Modacrylic fabrics are flame- and light-resistant and have good resistance to chemical stains. Otherwise they are quite similar to acrylics in their properties.

Nylon has high tensile strength, is slow to soil, and has good abrasion-resistance. However, it must be treated to prevent static electrical charge and is not very resistant to light.

Olefin has many of the qualities of wool, but at a much lower cost. It is stain-resistant and light in weight. On the negative side, olefin is heat-sensitive and collects static charge. It is also difficult to dye.

Polyester is crisp and resilient wet or dry, and wrinkle- and abrasion-resistant. As yarn, polyester tends to pill and collect static electricity. It is a fiber produced by many manufacturers under such well-known brand names as Dacron, Kodel, and Fortrel.

Saran fibers are not in very wide use for furnishings textiles. Saran does have good flame- and soil-resistance, and it is light and colorfast. However, it is rather heavy and heat-sensitive.

Aramid, Spandex, and vinyon are rarely used as furnishings textiles.

The above list of fibers includes the most important generic types in wide use by the textile industry making upholstery and drapery material. Fabrics identified by trade name usually identify fiber content. Some trade names relate clearly to the generic terms, such as Acrilan (made by Monsanto) does to acrylic. However, Orlon (made by du Pont) is in equally wide use and is not always identified as an acrylic fiber. Du Pont's Antron is often identified as "Antron-Nylon," which is indeed the proper fiber identification.

Fabric Production Methods

Weaves. Weaving is the interlacing of warp and filling yarns, usually at right angles to each other. The warp yarns run in the direction of manufacture on the loom, and the filling yarns (the weft or woof) interweave across the warp to fill and hold together the fabric. The three basic weaves are plain, twill, and satin.

The simplest form of plain weave is one in which the warp and filling yarns are identical in size and spacing so that they show equally on the face of the finished fabric. This balanced plain weave is also called broadcloth. Other plain weaves are rep and basket weaves, which are produced by interweaving relatively heavy yarns with thinner ones, or by crossing two or more warp yarns with two or more filling yarns to produce a distinct pattern.

Twill weave is one in which each woof or filling yarn "floats" across two or more warp yarns, causing a definite diagonal line (wale) on the fabric surface. Some typical twill fabrics are denim, gabardine, and serge. In comparison to plain weaves, twills are less likely to wrinkle and are more soil-resistant.

In satin weave, each warp yarn floats over four filling yarns. This reduces the over-and-under texture and results in smoother and more lustrous fabrics. Some typical satin weaves include satin, sateen, and damask.

TYPES OF WEAVE

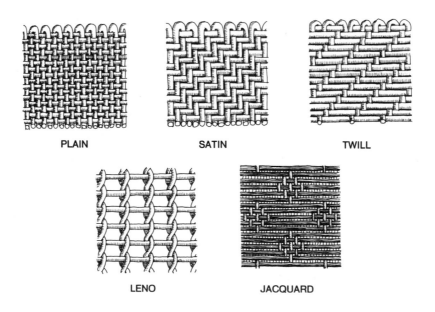

PLAIN   SATIN   TWILL

LENO   JACQUARD

Jacquard is a pattern weave produced on a very complex loom that is controlled by punch cards similar to those formerly used with computers. The most intricate patterns can be created on a jacquard loom, whether they be traditional damasks or brocades, or the most contemporary patterned textiles.

Pile weaves add a third element to the basic warp and filling in the form of yarns that project from the background. These create a fabric of greater thickness, with a surface formed of loops, as with terry cloth and frieze. When the loops are clipped, luxurious cloths such as velvet and velour are produced.

Lace weaves are created by crossing or twisting the warp yarns at various points to create an open, figured effect.

Nonwoven Fabrics. Felting is probably the earliest method of making cloth. It is simply the matting together of fibers to form a web. Normally wool is used for this process because of the tiny hooks along the length of its fibers. In the past, other hair was also used; today, blends with synthetics are common.

Knitting is a process using needles to interlock a continuous yarn into a series of interlaced loops. Many patterns are possible and a fabric of great flexibility and stretch is produced.

Plastic films result from processes such as extrusion, calendering, and casting. These produce sheets of material instead of filaments. Vinyl fabrics are an example of such manufacture. Knowledge of textiles helps in the appropriate specification of fabrics. However, selecting fibers, weaves, and patterns does not necessarily guarantee color stability, resistance to soil, and, above all, the degree of flammability. Color permanence is an important consideration for interior fabrics; some fade rapidly when exposed to strong light. Reputable textile manufacturers will choose dyes and chemical treatment carefully, employ expert dying techniques, and certify their products for colorfastness.

Standard tests for colorfastness have been established by the National Bureau of Standards. The astute specifier will ascertain that such certification has been obtained by the manufacturer. Fabrics for public buildings often must meet specific fire codes. The Boston Fire Code and the California Flammability Regulations are the most strict in the nation; they are likely to serve as models for the national standards. Manufacturers certify their fabrics with a fire rating, usually listing flame-spread and smoke-generation indexes. It may also be necessary to submit samples to the local fire departments for inspection and testing. Some fibers are inherently flame-resistant, but there are treatments and finishes to decrease flammability for most fabrics.

The maintenance factor must also be considered when specifying fabrics. Applied soil-resistant finishes can be of great service, but the intrinsic appropriateness of fiber and weave for specific applications must be given careful consideration.

Printing Fabrics. The most common method for applying patterns to cloth is roller printing as used for commercial production. Copper rollers, one for each color, deposit the pigments on the fabric. Variation of color can also be achieved by varying the depth of engraving on the roller, or by overprinting. Silk-screening used to be a hand process, but screen printing is less expensive as a production process. It is now possible to use automated screen printing, making this method yet more economical. Block printing is a manual technique, usually done with wood blocks, which are often surfaced with linoleum or metal.

Batik is a method in which part of the fabric is treated with wax to prevent dye from penetrating during the application of pigments. The process may be repeated with other pigments before removing the resist. A related technique is tie-dying, which uses ties and knots to prevent some of the fabric from accepting color when the material is immersed in dye. This results in diffuse, one-of-a-kind patterns.

Finishing Fabrics. Most fabrics receive some kind of finish after they are woven. Some chemical treatments, such as those that give fabric flame-retardance, soil-resistance, and water-repellency, are obvious in their intent and well known to the public. Other treatments protect against mildew and bacteria, improve insulation, reduce creasing, and reduce the discharge of static electricity.

Calendering refers to the process used to smooth and tighten weaves; it can also give fabrics a glazed sheen or polish. There are other finishes used by the textile industry to improve their process, but they are of little concern to the designer.

Drapery

Fabrics play an important role in window coverings, certainly much more than decoration. The purpose of curtains and draperies is manifold. Of the first importance is the control and modification of light. In many interiors it is desirable to filter strong daylight to reduce glare. Depending upon the climate and the orientation of the windows, a curtain may be a casement fabric filtering and softening the light or it may be a heavy fabric, often lined, that provides darkness and complete privacy at night. Frequently two layers of fabric are used: one to achieve softening of daylight, the other to control the light at night. Privacy is often achieved with fabrics, especially in residential interiors. Even in commercial uses where privacy is not generally of concern, casement or mesh window treatments are used much of the time.

Acoustics are another reason why fabrics are usually considered desirable across large expanses of glass. Many buildings of the last few decades have extensive glass areas. Unless curtains are used, along with carpeting and upholstered furniture, the sound in such spaces will be unpleasantly reverberant.

In recent years the insulating value of fabrics over windows has become more important. Thermal insulation is essential to energy-efficient buildings, and the easiest way to provide it is by use of appropriate fabrics in the form of draperies or shades. The insulation value of fabrics is equally valuable in blocking radiant heat from the sun or in keeping interiors warm. Heavy fabrics made into draperies with additional interlining can exclude or retain heat to an extensive degree. Fabrics can be tested and assigned a shading coefficient. This is a numerical percentage rating from 0 to 1.00 for light transmission in relation to temperature flow. The lower the number, the more efficient the fabric; .52 is considered effective.

Several aspects of window fabrics together create what is thought of as aesthetics. Color is the most noticeable feature relating to the purely visual effect of curtains. Since curtains, especially if installed floor to ceiling and wall to wall, represent one of the largest areas of color in any interior, the proper choice and combination of fabric colors can make or break a space. White and natural colors are very popular and indeed provide the best possible background for other colors. Of course it is possible to create very beautiful and exciting effects by using strongly colored fabrics as well. Another aesthetic consideration is the way draperies can be used to correct architectural problems such as projecting radiators, beams, and other eyesores. Frequently windows can be changed in their apparent size and proportion through the use of fabric curtains. Finally, carefully designed window treatments can enhance views to the outside or screen undesirable views.

In spite of the fact that the best window treatment may well be no treatment at all, where appropriate, draperies can become an important element in the hands of skilled design professionals.

Specifications. The single most important consideration in specifying window fabrics for proper performance is the flame-spread index. With the exception of glass fibers, there are no completely fireproof fabrics. (Asbestos is also fireproof but is not practical for normal use.) Since the National Life Safety Code is not uniformly adopted, it is necessary that specifiers ascertain with their local fire marshal what kind of fabrics may be used in buildings for public use. It may be necessary to submit actual fabric samples to the local department for flammability tests. Fabrics of high flame-spread or smoke-generation index should never be used in buildings for public use, and it is advisable to avoid them even in private residences. It is possible to treat almost any fabric with fire-retardant finishes. Some finishes are more durable than others; the standard is defined as one that will last through twenty-five washings or twenty dry cleanings. Some fabrics are rated as being inherently flame-resistant, which means that they do not ignite readily and burn slowly if ignited. Included in this category are wools and silks among natural fibers, and nylons, olefins, and polyesters among the synthetics. Fire-retardant fibers include modacrylics and sarans; however, it is important to differentiate this lesser category from flame-resistant fabrics.

Dimensional stability is a highly desirable characteristic of window fabrics. Sagging and shrinking as the result of humidity changes is the most frequent cause for complaint in poorly specified curtains. Most fabrics tend to sag over a long period of time; while a 2 percent change may be tolerable, some fabrics may sag considerably more than that. Shrinking is often the result of washing, but many fabrics are available preshrunk.

All but mineral fibers are subject to some deterioration when exposed to direct sunlight. Silk, for instance, without lining or shades to protect it from the sun, will deteriorate very rapidly. It is important, therefore, to protect window fabrics, especially if costly materials have been specified.

Fabrics are also subject to mildew, especially in humid climates. In addition to selection of fabrics with natural resistance to mildew, it is possible to have any fabric treated with special protective finishes.

(For more information on specifications, see *Specifications for Commercial Interiors, Revised* by S. C. Reznikoff [Whitney Library of Design, 1989.])

Upholstery

The choice of upholstery fabrics is almost limitless. The range of designs, weaves, textures, and colors available is one of the most exciting design factors for interior designers and the public. Upholstery fabrics can change the appearance of furniture, and, more than any other element in an interior, can provide color accent and create the total mood and atmosphere of a space. As a consequence, such fabrics must be carefully specified; the wrong fabric can be detrimental to an otherwise carefully planned space. Fabrics that are not meant for heavy-duty use may quickly become worn. Other fabrics can easily soil, and even the wrong color selection can cause maintenance difficulties.

The appearance of fabrics must be considered in terms of scale. For instance, large patterns are usually wrong for small and delicate pieces of furniture. The sense of touch is also important. A smooth wool fabric may have a far more pleasant hand that a roughly textured mixture of wool and synthetics. The tactile sense is especially important during the summer months when people are lightly clad. Chair upholstery can be exceedingly uncomfortable during hot weather if the fabric is sheet plastic; fabrics that are porous are particularly important in warmer climates.

Durability is an important quality expected from upholstery fabrics. However, life expectancy should not be the only criterion in selecting and specifying fabrics; the appearance, hand, and other comfort considerations must not be overlooked. Pilling and snagging are two problems that affect the endurance of certain fabrics. Pilling occurs most frequently in new wool fabrics but diminishes with time. It refers to fibers coming loose from the fabric surface and forming balls. It is most noticeable in carpets, but pilling will have a detrimental effect on upholstery. Snagging refers to yarns that pull from the surface and catch in clothing or objects.

One of the key factors in fabric wear is abrasion. The areas that receive the most abrasion on upholstered pieces always show wear first. Testing for abrasion-resistance is possible and may be requested of the manufacturer by the specifier for major installations. Abrasion may also cause loss of color if the dye has not properly penetrated the fabric.

Dimensional stability is extremely important to upholstery fabrics. Wrinkling or sagging occurs when the fabric does not have enough resilience. There are special stretch fabrics for highly contoured furniture, and in many cases manufacturers of furniture with sculptural forms will only use fabrics that have been especially selected for such pieces.

Specification of fabrics requires a fair amount of knowledge about textiles. Above all, it requires the understanding that the counsel of experts may need to be sought. Reputable manufacturers usually label their fabrics clearly with fiber content and special features or treatment. If this is not done, the pertinent information should be obtained from the manufacturer.

Specifications involve a good deal of common sense. Upholstery fabrics need to be tough and durable, much more so than those for drapery. They will be heavier in weight and more tightly woven. For heavy-duty use, nylons and wools or a blend of these fibers are likely to be durable. Fabrics that are selected for aesthetic considerations alone may only do half the job. Each project will have different criteria for fabrics; the intended use of the space and the furniture selected will determine the best fabrics choice.

The sensitivity required to understand the successful balance between practical demands and aesthetic desires must be carefully cultivated. When you are not sure of the best choice among fabrics, it is wiser to seek the advice of the manufacturer than to assume responsibility without knowing all the pertinent facts.

14 Rugs and Carpets

Carpeting is a heavy woven or felted fabric used as a floorcovering. In modern usage, carpeting often, but not necessarily, covers the floor to the walls.

A rug is a piece of heavy fabric, usually with a pile, that is used for a floorcovering. Modern usage considers a rug as a floor element that does not usually cover the entire floor.

Despite the usages suggested here, the terms carpeting and rug are often interchangeable.

The earliest known woven floorcoverings appeared in the Far East and Egypt about 3000 B.C. It is believed that rugs are a product of Egyptian influence that spread through the Middle East and beyond, to Mongolia and China. Others believe that, ultimately, the origin of all carpets can be traced to Central Asia. From the Medieval period, Oriental rugs were imported by merchants to Europe, where they were principally used as wall hangings.

In Spain, carpet making was practiced as a Moorish art from as early as the twelfth century. Manufacture was started in the sixteenth century in both England and France, and by the eighteenth century, centers for carpet making developed in England at Wilton and Axminster. The invention of the Jacquard mechanism in the nineteenth century developed the full industrial production of carpets. By this time the United States had adopted the British carpet-making system, and rug mills were established in several eastern states. It was not until the end of World War II that needle tufting was developed, permitting the carpet industry to rapidly evolve into the present mode of production.

Types of Carpeting

The nomenclature of carpeting is based upon a number of elements: the method of construction, the materials used, the pattern and texture of the surface, and the finished size. Size often establishes the difference between area rugs and wall-to-wall carpeting. Sometimes the attempt is made to distinguish between area rugs and scatter rugs. The latter would be relatively smaller than area rugs and used mostly for decorative purposes. The smallest unit of carpeting is the carpet tile, but these are made to be joined to form a larger unit.

All historic carpets are area rugs. The best, such as antique Oriental rugs, are hand made, and they are still being made by hand today. Some beautiful Oriental rugs are accepted and priced as works of art. The most frequently used material was, and still is, wool; but silk, or a combination of silk and wool, has been extensively used.

Wall-to-wall carpeting became popular only after the end of World War II. The circumstances of the war brought about a shortage of wool, while technology engendered the development of a variety of synthetic fibers that proved to be suitable for carpeting.

Carpet Weaves. The four traditional weaves for carpeting are Wilton, velvet, Axminster, and chenille. The factors that determine the weave in carpet manufacture are the pitch, the pile height, and the ply of the yarn. Pitch is the number of face yarns per inch; pile height is the height of the yarn above the backing; and the ply is the number of individual ends of yarn twisted together.

Wilton and Axminster weaves are named after the English towns where they were first produced. Wilton is a modification of the Jacquard system that makes it possible to produce the most intricate patterns. The different colors are usually visible on the back. The Axminster system simulates hand weaving by inserting each tuft individually. The backing is so heavily sized that it can only be rolled out lengthwise. Velvet weave is formed by looping the pile over wires inserted above the warp. The wires are pulled to cut the loops. Velvet is suitable only for solid colors, unless yarns of different colors are twisted to produce tweeds. Chenille is a system of tufting that leaves uncut piles projecting from the backing.

Tufting is a newer process that probably accounts for 70 percent of the carpeting mass-produced today. Yarns are needled through the backing by a less costly process than weaving. Essentially, tufting machines are similar to sewing machines, except that instead of a single needle, a tufting machine has hundreds or even thousands of needles. Tufted carpets were originally solid color or tweeds, using colored yarns or yarns dyed after weaving. With the introduction of electronic controls to tufting machines, almost unlimited textures and patterns are possible. To anchor the tufts an additional backing is cemented to the base, and often a foam backing is applied.

Other manufacturing processes include needle punching, knitting, and custom tufting. Needle punching is an inexpensive process that presses unspun fibers through a woven sheet, resulting in a feltlike product. By using synthetic fibers not subject to decay, the indoor-outdoor carpet is produced. The knitted carpet, unlike the woven carpet, loops together the backing, stitching, and pile yarns in one operation, using needles as in hand knitting. Custom tufting approaches the handwoven carpet in design, flexibility, and cost.

CARPET PILE AND PITCH

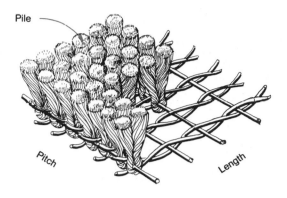

Pile

Pitch

Length

CARPET CONSTRUCTION

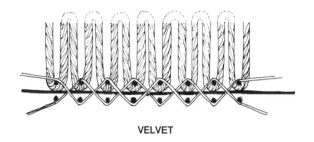

VELVET

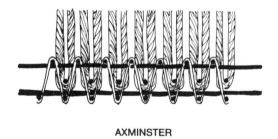

AXMINSTER

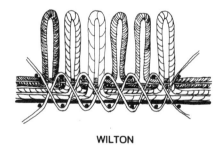

WILTON

TUFTED CARPET

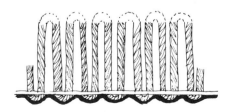

Quality Factors

The prime determinate of carpet performance is the density of the pile, that is, the amount of pile yarn in a given area of the carpet face. Since the cost of carpeting is also influenced by the amount of surface material in its height and density, a formula useful to specifiers of carpet is:

$$\text{density/sq. yd.} = \frac{36 \times \text{pile weight (oz./sq. yd.)}}{\text{pile height (inches)}}$$

This formula shows that a 30 oz./sq. yd. carpet with a ½-inch-thick pile has a density of 2160. A carpet of the same weight with a ¾-inch pile has a density of only 1440.

The pitch and size of the yarns are also important quality factors. Pitch represents the number of pile yarns in a given width; the higher the number, the denser the carpet. The longer the yarn for a given pitch, the denser and heavier the carpet.

Backings are another quality determinate. In woven and knitted carpeting, backing yarns and pile yarns are combined during the fabric-formation process. For these weaves today, polypropylene is the material most frequently used for backing, although fibers such as jute, rayon, linen, and polyester are still in common use.

Preformed backings are necessary for tufted carpets, for there must be material into which to tuft the pile yarns. Following the weaving and dying processes, a secondary backing is usually applied. One of three methods completes the manufacturing process: lamination of a secondary fabric backing, coating with synthetic latex or another polymer, or the application of a synthetic-latex foam cushion. For needle-punched carpets the most frequently used backing is synthetic-rubber latex. These secondary backings immeasurably improve the dimensional stability and provide greater resistance to stretching and wrinkling under heavy traffic.

Carpet weight and pile height are usually specified for the tufting machine. The total finished carpet weight should be included in the specifications. The figure should not be confused with pile yarn weight. The total finished weight includes all backing materials, foams, latexes, finishes, and face yarns. While this total weight cannot be the only determinate of quality, for comparison with another carpet of a given size and manufacture it is a good indicator. In velvet-weave carpet, pile height is stated by wire size, the height of the steel blades in a loom on which the pile is formed. If the given wire height is 0.250 inches (6 mm), the pile height will be approximately ¼ inch (6 mm). Pile heights of tufted carpets are expressed as either fractions or decimals of an inch.

Pile Fibers and Yarns. Most commercial carpets are manufactured from the following five pile fibers: acrylic (including modacrylic blends), nylon, olefin, polyester, and wool.

Some cotton is used, but for residential carpeting only. If appearance were the only factor determining specifications, wool would be the preferred fiber for most designers. Wool is also an extremely strong fiber that can withstand a great deal of wear and tear. There are woolen Oriental rugs that have been in use for many decades, and some of them have survived for hundreds of years. Clearly these are very tightly woven rugs, but this does demonstrate the inherent strength and permanence of wool, as well as its beauty.

All of the other fibers listed are synthetic fibers, which may be crimped or textured to increase their bulk and covering power. They may be cut into short staples and spun like wool, or used as continuous filaments. Acrylics and modacrylics are the synthetics that most resemble wool in abrasion-resistance and texture. Nylon comprises nearly half of all the yardage of carpet used today. It is lower in cost than most other fibers, is durable, and is available in strong colors. Olefin has the lowest moisture-absorption rate, which makes it the most stain-resistant and washable fabric. While light in weight, it has good wear-resistance. Polyester is resilient and wear-resistant, but it is less commonly used in carpet manufacture than the other synthetics listed.

The manufacturer's recommendations for the appropriate application of fibers should be consulted before specifying a rug or carpet. These recommendations take into consideration the total composition of their product, and are based upon extensive testing. Often yarn type and size are particularly specified in contract carpeting. Yarn size is specified as cotton count or denier and is an indication of the degree of firmness. Cotton count is used for spun yarns and denier for continuous-filament yarns.

Cotton count is defined as the number of skeins, 840 yards (770 meters), of yarn in one pound (454 grams). The larger the cotton-count number, the finer the yarn. In the United States, the denier system is used to define the size of continuous filament yarns, such as BFC nylon carpet yarns. Denier is the weight in grams of 9,000 meters of yarn. The lower the denier, the finer the yarn. There are formulas for the specifier who must choose between spun and continuous filament yarns and who must distinguish the relationship between spun yarns expressed in cotton count and filament size noted in denier. Further properties of these fibers may be found in the chapter on textiles.

Flammability. The number of fires in hotels and other public spaces in recent years has raised a great deal of concern about the flammability and smoke generation of building materials, including carpeting. Most carpeting comes with precise manufacturer's specifications including the flammability rating by letter code or by American Society for Testing Materials (ASTM) ratings. Aside from the designer's personal commitment to public safety, there are building-code requirements that must be followed. Not all building codes are the same, and it is necessary for the designer to consult the building code adopted by the governmental body that has jurisdiction over the project. Probably California and the city of Boston have the most stringent flammability codes at the present time. For example, in addition to high performance standards, the fire department of Boston requires the submission of actual samples of the material before approval is given for installation. The Federal Standard FF 1–70 controls carpet manufactured in the United States under the Flammability Fabrics Act. The National Institute for Standards and Technology (formerly National Bureau of Standards) continues to develop new standards, especially for installations such as hotels, hospitals, and places of public assembly. Trade associations continuously research to develop new products with better safety factors. (For additional information see *Specification for Commercial Interiors, Revised* by S. C. Reznikoff [Whitney Library of Design, 1989.])

Another aspect of flammability and smoke generation associated with carpeting is the behavior of materials in the presence of a fully developed fire, where intense heat is radiated to the floor. Standard tests, such as the Steiner Tunnel Test, have been developed to establish ratings for specific carpets.

Typical information available for a carpet from a reputable manufacturer will include the following:

Name and quality: manufacturer's designation
Construction: e.g., "tufted level loop pile"
Yarn: e.g., "3-ply woolen fiber 5% wool, 45% acrylic"
Coloration: e.g., "dyed," "natural," etc.
Gauge: e.g., "⅛″ = equivalent 216 pitch"
Stitches per 6″: e.g., "41"
Pile height: e.g., "⅛," "⁹⁄₃₂," etc.
Face weight: e.g., "32 oz./sq. yd."
Primary back: e.g., "polypropylene"
Secondary back: e.g., "jute"
Static control: e.g., "permanent static control"
Flame spread: e.g., "ASTM-E84: passed class B," "41"
Fuel contributed factor: e.g., "43"
Smoke-density factor: e.g., "244"

The listing of the smoke-density factor shows the growing concern for more than mere flammability. Some materials are not flammable, but will burn in the presence of fire. Others may not be highly flammable but will give off quantities of smoke, which may be highly toxic.

Static Control. Static electricity may be a serious problem with carpeting, especially in winter when the interior humidity is likely to be low. People gain an electric charge when walking over carpet; this charge is then discharged to the next thing that is touched, especially if it is metallic. Static discharge can be a serious problem in spaces where computers or other sensitive electronic equipment is housed.

Despite advertising copy, no carpet is completely static-free. There are static inhibitors built into carpets, including metallic threads woven into the material to continuously drain the charge. Other methods to reduce static include using special coatings on fibers, specific blends, and engineered fibers. Nylon, polyester, and wool seem to generate more static electricity than acrylic and olefin. The proper choice of carpet, together with humidity control, can provide an environment almost free of static charge. For existing carpets, sprays and powders are available that help; these may be the only solution in spaces where the humidity level cannot be controlled.

In spaces where static discharge may be dangerous, such as an operating room where nitrous oxide is present, carpet is simply not the appropriate flooring material.

Acoustical Control. Carpets are a most useful sound-control device. They are the only excellent floorcovering that provides acoustical benefits as well. It is doubtful that the popular open plan for offices could ever have been developed without the appearance of wall-to-wall carpeting. Years earlier, carpets revolutionized school design by permitting the introduction of the open classroom. Carpet not only absorbs reverberation within a space, it reduces sound from the source by deadening footfalls. This is equally valuable in preventing the transmission of sound to the floor below.

By testing materials for sound absorption, a noise reduction coefficient (NRC) is assigned. Carpets with a pile height from ⅛″ to 7/17″ (3 to 11 mm) have an NCR rating from .15 to .40. This is good enough to encourage the use of carpet as a wall material, where it provides a long-lasting, low-maintenance surface.

Specifications

The vast amount of choice available to the designer makes proper specifications difficult and important. In the field of specifications there are two basic types: performance and construction. Performance specifications spell out what the carpet is expected to do, but do not tell the manufacturer how it is to be made. They may specify that the color must be resistant to fading, or the amount of static charge that may be permissible. Since designers cannot be totally familiar with the latest fabrication technology, performance specification is easier than construction specification. Whatever code requirements apply can be spelled out, putting the burden of compliance on the manufacturer. Performance specifications must be written in accordance with standards the industry has adopted.

Construction specifications must call for the type of construction, such as woven or tufted. This is followed by a list of such information as gauge (pitch), stitches per inch, fiber, face weight per square yard, pile height, yarn ply and count, backing material and coating, and finished weight per square yard. Frequently construction specifications refer to a specific carpet by trade name and manufacturer. If the specification is followed by the term "or equal," the bidder has the choice of using other, similar products.

Specifications may also include the method of installation and, if the installation is tackless, the kind of underlayment. Specifiers should require certification that materials meet the various code requirements. It is usually necessary to include delivery schedules and installation dates, especially on commercial projects.

Before the actual selection and specification, the designer needs to resolve some basic questions regarding the budget, the design and color of the carpet, the severity of the traffic load, the minimum life expectancy, and any special installation requirements. Reputable carpet dealers will help the specifier by sharing their experience and all the technical information available from the manufacturer.

Installation

The two main methods for wall-to-wall carpet installation are the "stretched-in" method, on tackless strips, and the "glue-down" method. Tackless installations (for carpet that at some time had been tacked down) should be done over carpet pads or underlayments of felt or foam rubber. The pad enhances the wear capability of the carpet and provides a softer, more luxurious effect.

TACKLESS CARPET INSTALLATION

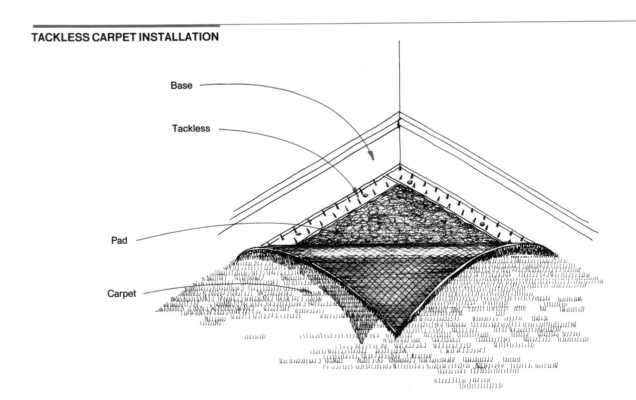

Base

Tackless

Pad

Carpet

The majority of carpets in commercial installations today are put down as a glue-down installation. The carpet may have an attached foam padding, or the backing may be glued directly to the flooring. The latter is not as soft underfoot but works well for areas where very heavy, or rolling, traffic is expected. Glue-down installations are possible for most types of underlayment: concrete, wood, or ceramic tile. This system causes few problems where the adequate amount of the correct adhesive is used according to specifications. With the glue-down method, repairs are easily accomplished by cutting out the damaged area and gluing down scraps saved from the original installation.

Tackless strip installations must be carefully done by competent mechanics. If the carpet has not been properly stretched, it will soon bag. Some carpets, particularly those of wool, will need to be restretched after a period of time. Professional installers usually allow for this in their original cost estimate. Although carpeting is available in widths as great as 20 feet (6 m), seams will occur, and these must be made carefully. Most installers use hot-melt seam tapes, which seem to be satisfactory.

Maintenance

Interior designers are not ordinarily involved with maintenance programs for the spaces they design. For carpeting, however, it is wise to see that the client is aware of proper maintenance procedures. Regardless of the job conditions or the dirt that may be brought in from an adjacent area, if the carpets do not stand up as expected, the blame falls on the designer.

Carpets in high-traffic areas must be vacuumed daily, and even in moderately busy areas, twice weekly. Dirt in the pile of the carpet is more than unsightly; it contributes to the premature abrasion of the yarns. Poorly maintained carpet looks worn because the face fibers become matted down. Whether the carpets are actually worn or only look worn matters little; they will need replacement in either case.

When selecting carpet, designers must carefully consider the color and texture in terms of maintenance. Delicate colors are not suitable for high-traffic areas. Often the tweed mixture of colors, despite the preferences of the designer, may be the only proper solution. Patterned carpets may be preferred by restaurants and hotels as a protection against the appearance of dirt and stains.

At entrances it is best to specify foul-weather mats; vestibules and elevators should also have special provisions, such as cocoa matting. Two sets of mats are best; one set can be used while the other is being cleaned. In offices, chair pads are often provided, although many new office chairs have casters designed for use on carpeted floors.

Aside from vacuuming, carpets and rugs should be cleaned periodically. Professional cleaning services use chemical methods, wet extraction, or whatever system is most suitable. There are effective chemical protective treatments that can keep carpets from prematurely soiling and can prolong their life. In spite of all efforts, however, carpeting will not last forever, especially in high-traffic areas. Clients should recognize this, and it is well for the designer to emphasize this from the beginning.

Carpet tiles serve well in spaces where spillage or exceptionally high traffic is expected. They are easy to replace or rearrange before wear shows.

While many of these considerations are aimed at contract installations, residential work is a large segment of the field of interior design. High-pile carpets are seldom used in commercial spaces, but are very popular in the home. While Oriental rugs are mostly used for residential applications, in executive offices they can give a sense of elegance and luxury that may be worth the cost. Most of the criteria for commercial work will apply to residences. Because the quantities involved are usually much smaller, the designer's responsibilities are less severe.

Whether for residential or commercial use, carpeting represents an important tool in the hands of the designer.

Index